The Reviews Are In...

"As a sales psychologist I have seen sales professionals lose very large commissions due to weak voices and what clients perceived as a lack of enthusiasm. This book contains wisdom that, if used, will put thousands of dollars of extra income into the pockets of readers."
~Donald J. Moine, Ph.D, president, Association for Human Achievement, Inc. author "Unlimited Selling Power"

"I learned a lot that was original and new to me. Susan Berkley knows her stuff—she shows you how to bring out the power and the glory of your voice."
~Burt Dubin, creator of "The Speaking Success System"

"Speak To Influence opened my eyes and my voice! Susan Berkley's practical exercises produced immediate changes in my unconscious bad habits hardened by years of lecturing. A must read for educators."
~Jonathan Montaldo, lecturer, writer and editor "The Journals of Thomas Merton"

"Speak To Influence provides vital information for busy MBA students who don't have time to plow through a theoretical tome. I adopted this book for my course because of the warm, upbeat tone and practical tips."
~Susan Mach, Ph.D, adjunct management communication professor Stern School of Business, New York University

"I never realized my voice could win friends and influence people until I read this book. It contains the inner secrets of vocal persuasion—an art nobody knows as well as the master, Susan Berkley."
~Joe Vitale, author, "There's a Customer Born Every Minute"

"Speak to Influence is a 'must read' for anyone who wants to communicate with confidence and power."
~Gerri Detweiler, speaker, consultant author, "The Ultimate Credit Handbook"

"The tips, tactics, and tremendous ideas for content and delivery in Susan's book will have them standing up and applauding for more. A must for every speaker—even the pros."

~Bernard Hale Zick, CEO,
The Intl. Society of Speakers, Authors, & Consultants

"A fantastic recipe for vocal success."

~Jay Morris & Michael Vitale
WQXC – Kalamazoo, MI

"I teach that good promotion and good speaking go hand in hand. So I highly recommend *Speak To Influence* to any one who wants to maximize their marketing and publicity efforts."

~Raleigh Pinskey,
author, "101 Ways To Promote Yourself"

" This book is a must for anyone who is in the public eye. I use these techniques daily to help keep people animated and interested. The broadcasters tips help make the work I do that much more powerful."

~Marc Streisand, president
Inside Out Image Consulting

"Susan covers everything from emotional to physical factors that can make or break your voice. Use these techniques and reap the rewards."

~Noah St. John, seminar leader
author, "Permission to Succeed"

"Good, practical tips you can use immediately for anyone who wants to improve their voice. A great book to take on the road"

Diane DiResta, president DiResta Communications
author, "Knockout Presentations"

"A winner! Susan had the power of persuasion over me!"

~Brian Nuttall, host of "The Experts"
CFPL - London, Ontario Canada

SPEAK to Influence

How to Unlock the Hidden Power of Your Voice

Susan Berkley

CAMPBELL
HALL
PRESS

Englewood Cliffs, New Jersey

Speak To Influence
How to Unlock the Hidden Power of Your Voice

By Susan Berkley

For more information contact:

 Campbell Hall Press
616 East Palisade Avenue
Englewood Cliffs, New Jersey 07632
(201) 541-8595
http://www.greatvoice.com

ISBN 0-9664302-1-2
Library of Congress Catalog Card Number: 98-96218

9 8 7 6 5 4 3 2

Printed in the United States of America

Publishers note
This publication is designed to provide accurate and authoritative information in regard to the subject matter covered. It is sold with the understanding that the publisher is not engaged in rendering legal, accounting, or other professional service. If legal or medical advice or other expert assistance is required, the services of a competent professional should be sought.

The purpose of this book is to educate and entertain. The author and Campbell Hall Press shall have neither liability nor responsibility to any person or entity with respect to any loss or damage caused, or alleged to be caused, directly or indirectly, by the information contained in this book.

If you do not wish to be bound by the above you may return this book to the publisher for a complete refund.

This book is dedicated with deepest gratitude to:

Dr. Norberto R. Keppe and Dr. Claudia B. Pacheco

Your input was vital in helping me to understand
the emotional roots of speech fright
and to separate the essentials of
good communication from the particulars.
Because of your work and dedication, your
inspiration and guidance, so many of us are leading
happier, healthier, more meaningful lives.

Acknowledgments

Heartfelt thanks to:

Everyone who has participated in my workshops and teleclasses.
Victoria Memminger: for first-class editorial help
Liz de Nesnera: for layout, design and for overall brilliance and support.
Scott Kastner: webmaster and studio engineer extraordinaire.
Mia Diaz: Public Relations and fulfillment
Liz, Scott and Mia - I am truly blessed to have you on my team
My friends at Millenium in Sao Paulo
Judy Robinett: for your vision, caring and insight
Hilton and Lisa Johnson: for guidance and friendship
Joe Vitale, Susan Mach, Gerri Detweiler, Jim and Audri Lanford, John
Iams, David Deutsch, Karen Anderson, Parris Lampropolous, Joel
Roberts and Rick Popowitz: for being so supportive and generous with
your ideas and your time.
Special thanks to Dr. Donald Moine, Dr. Wallace Rubin, Todd Taccetta
Design, Bernard Hale Zick, and Valerie Geller, author of *Creating
Powerful Radio* (www.gellermedia.com)
And to: Diana Boyleston and Wesley Clark for your precious
friendship.
With love to my family and to my husband Ron, whose golden voice
makes my heart sing.

Photo credit: Tania Mara
Cover design: Lightbourne Images
Text layout/design: Liz de Nesnera
Editorial: Victoria Memminger, Barbara Brent, Bruce Tracy

Contents

Read This First . . .

I recently heard some startling information about first impressions. If you don't make a favorable one within the first twelve seconds, you must make seven subsequent positive impressions to undo the damage done the first time around.

But there's a myth out there about first impressions. It goes something like this. To succeed in life, all you need is a shiny image and the right technique. Get good and shiny enough, master all the details and doors that were previously shut will magically open; men and women will kiss your feet and you'll be able to convince anyone to do your bidding.

I would like to dispel this myth right now. When someone gives a memorable talk, we don't remember the speaker because of the particulars of their speech- their hand gestures, vocal inflection or perfect hair. We remember them because of the essence of their talk and because they touched something deep and meaningful within our soul.

Yes, this is practical handbook, a compendium of voice mastery techniques. But these techniques, the particulars of speaking, will fall short of giving you the results you want if you speak without being grounded in positive intention.

I believe that deep within us all is an essence that is good, beautiful and true. Align yourself with this essence and your words become powerful indeed. Neglect this important first step and your presentation will be just another talk. Pretty to listen to maybe, but easily forgotten and sorely lacking in motivational power.

So what does it mean to speak with good intention in alignment with your essence? It can be as simple as the desire to share information, clarify a process, enlighten, inform or entertain. Or it can be as lofty as a desire to denounce an injustice or bring peace and freedom to the world.

Intention is potent force. It's the X-Factor, the charisma, the "special sauce" behind the speech. When you are aligned with a positive intention, your message is memorable and can even have the potential to make history. Think JFK, Winston Churchill and Dr. Martin Luther King. And think *you* at your most inspired.

People are incredibly adept at capturing our intention whenever they size us up. Psychologists tell us that first impressions are correct 67% of the time. But even if you manage to fool some of the people some of the time, in the end, your intention will ultimately lift you to the top or plunge you into ruin (Hitler, cult leader Jim Jones).

Ultimately, intentions and technique work hand in hand in everything we do. A lawyer with bad intentions and great technique may help a guilty psychopath walk free. A doctor with good intentions and no technique might have a great bedside manner but kill the patient. And a speaker with good intentions but no technique—someone, for example, who is difficult to understand—may end up putting the audience to sleep.

Get in touch with the **essentials** of your message and the particulars of delivering it will be that much easier to master. The most powerful essential is love. Touch the heart of the listener and they'll barely notice if your voice is less than mellifluous or if your hand gestures are a little too choppy. In fact, many communication problems are caused because the speaker is temporarily out of touch with their essence. A monotonous speaker has lost touch with his essential enthusiasm. A dry, humorless speaker has temporarily lost touch with his essential joy. A theoretical speaker has lost touch with his humanity.

Several techniques are effective in helping to get grounded in the essentials before speaking. These include reading inspirational literature, listening to uplifting music and spending time in nature.

Like any great performer, a speaker seeks to attain a state of grace where he is in perfect synch with the audience. These are rare moments where we say the perfect thing at the perfect time and inspiration seems to flow effortlessly from our mouth. Ironically, when these moments happen, we often don't know how or why. But what I do know is that moments of magic don't occur when we are flawless. They occur when we are grounded in a positive intention, when we are prepared, and when we have heart.

Vocal charisma, then, is what happens when heart meets technique.

1

What This Book Can Do For You

No matter what you do for a living, your voice and the way you use it is as essential to you as to an opera singer. Yet most people barely give their voice a second thought, let alone investing the time needed to learn how to improve it or use it to maximum effect.

This is not just a problem in business, it's a problem everywhere in America today. The sound of America is deteriorating rapidly. Speech and debating classes have gone the way of the horse and buggy. Gone, too, are the classically trained actors whose beautiful, resonant voices were a hallmark of old movies. Movie stars today might look good, but their voices are often flat, forgettable, and monotonous. Even President Clinton is frequently in vocal distress; his weak, raspy voice makes you wonder if every speech he gives will be his last.

As for the rest of the populace, we seem to be growing more and more inarticulate, whiney, and sloppy about our speech. In many places, just asking for directions becomes a challenge, since you can find yourself trying to decipher both mumbling and a regional accent. These two vocal off-putters, by the way, are high on the list of what annoys people about other people's voices. A Gallup poll that surveyed 500 men and women on this subject put mumbling or talking too softly at the top of the list. These were followed by yelling; speaking in a monotone; using vocal fillers such as "um," "like" or "you know;" a whiney, nasal voice; talking too fast; poor grammar; a high-pitched voice; a foreign accent or regional dialect that is all but impossible to understand.

How Do You Measure Up?

Are you afflicted with any of these vocal no-no's? Could you inadvertently be turning people off every time you speak? It's hard to believe, but when you talk to someone on the phone who has never met you, within the first 30 seconds of hearing your voice the other person has formed a mental image of you: what you look like, how smart you are, and whether or not they are going to listen to what you have to say.

What does this mean? It means the sound of your voice can have a direct relationship to the size of your bank account.

That's because in today's telephone-intensive world, almost every business relationship starts over the telephone. And many stay there. If you're like I am, you have clients or customers you have never met—people who know you only by the sound of your voice. In fact, you probably have a few important customers you wouldn't recognize even if you were standing next to them in a crowded elevator. Until, that is, you heard them speak.

Whenever you speak, the sound of your voice generates emotions, feelings, and gut-level reactions in other people. Some of these emotions are conscious and some are not, but these gut-level reactions form the basis for whether or not people like you, trust you, never take your call again, or decide to do business with you in the future.

You have probably heard a million times that people buy on emotion but justify with fact. Well, your voice is the most powerful tool you've got for generating emotions in another person. When you master the art of using your voice, you vastly improve your ability to give people positive, gut-level hunches about you, your client, your product or service. I call this vital skill "hunch power."

In the first few weeks of life, before we can focus our eyes or understand language, we sense the relative safety of our environment by the tone of the voices around us. If the voices sound warm and nurturing, we feel safe and loved. If they sound harsh or annoying, we feel threatened and afraid. Some studies show that babies even respond to voices while they are still in the womb.

In the chapters that follow, you'll learn how to use your voice to give people positive gut-level feelings about you. This is a critical skill.

If the person you are talking to senses any kind of threat or annoyance in the tone of your voice, if they perceive any incongruence between your body language, tone of voice, or spoken words, you just won't get through. No matter what words you use, you won't be believed—and you won't be trusted.

Never Underestimate The Power Of . . . Your Voice

Did you know that how you sound affects how attractive you seem? Speech consultant Dr. Lillian Glass did a fascinating study showing how speech affects perceived attractiveness. She paired photographs of good looking people, average people, and people with facial deformities with tape recorded speech samples of voices that were normal, mildly nasal, and severely nasal.

After analyzing subjects' reactions to the different combinations of faces and voices, Dr. Glass found that the facially deformed subjects were considered more attractive when paired with a pleasant voice than when paired with a nasal speaking voice. Conversely, good looking people with nasal speech were considered unattractive, even though they had been judged attractive when paired with non-nasal speech. Not only does this study show that people judge us by the way we speak—it shows we can actually improve our perceived appearance just by improving the sound of our voice.

In Case You're Looking For Statistics . . .

Many people think that communicating effectively is merely a matter of finding and using the right magic words. They believe that using certain words in the right order will get them the results they want. Unfortunately, these people are living in a dream world. Scientific research tells us that attempting to persuade by words alone is about as effective as trying to chop down a tree with a Swiss Army knife. To be a truly effective communicator, your body language and tone of voice must be consistent with your content. Even the most powerful words spoken in a monotone with lifeless body language will fail to rouse anyone. In a study conducted at UCLA, Dr. Albert Mehrabian found that when verbal, vocal and visual signals are inconsistent, content counts for a mere seven percent of the overall message. In such a situation, 55 percent of the message is transmitted by facial expression and body language; and 38 percent comes from voice quality—pitch, tone, volume, and inflection.

Think about it: If you've been given the luxury of "face time" with a person you want to influence, a warm, friendly smile, a firm handshake, and good eye-contact can work wonders. But if anything about your voice is flat or distracting, annoying or boring, you've just reduced your effectiveness by 38 percent.

And how often do we spend face-to-face time with our customers in these days of phone-computer-fax? So. . .discounting the attractive physical impression (until the days of picture-phone are truly with us), what counts is not only what you say, but how you say it.

Dr. Mehrabian's research bears this out. He found that when talking on the phone, the actual words you use account for only 16 percent of the way you—and the products and services you represent—are perceived. The remaining 84 percent of your impression depends on the sound of your voice and the feelings people get when listening to you.

What This Book Will Do For You

It will make you a more persuasive person. It will help you sell more products and services and make a lasting and favorable first impression. I know what I'm talking about—I am a professional voice-over artist. My voice has helped my clients sell millions of dollars worth of products and corporate services. You've heard me on television, radio, and telephone. In fact, mine is one of the voices that says "Thank you for using. . .," the services of a major telecommunications company.

This book will teach you the previously unrevealed speaking secrets of America's most compelling, persuasive, and highly paid voices—so you can use these secrets to become a more effective communicator in your professional and personal life.

For instance...

• You'll learn how to speak with more energy, emotion, and enthusiasm. We'll work on posture and body language and discover the tremendous effect your physical being has on the way you speak.

• You'll learn how to cure yourself of what I call the "verbal viruses." Verbal viruses are distracting non-words and phrases such as "like," "I mean," "ummm," or "ahhhh."

• You'll learn how breathing affects the voice. And what proper breathing can and cannot do to make you a more effective speaker.

- You'll learn how to sound more credible and learn why it's not what you say, but how you say it that counts.

- You'll discover how to add more music to your speech by mastering vocal pitch, tone, and inflection.

- You'll see how rate of speech affects selling ability and you'll develop a richer, more resonant tone through vocal placement.

- You'll learn to change the tone of your voice at will, match and mirror other people's voices for better rapport, and use your voice to express the full range of emotions, from warm and friendly to energetic, enthusiastic, and passionate.

- You'll find out how to get your ideas across in a more interesting manner and how to tell great stories.

- You'll discover how to say the right thing at precisely the right time; how to communicate with greater diplomacy, tact, and charm.

- You'll learn the secrets of stress-free speaking.

By the time you finish this book, you will have vastly improved your ability to express yourself credibly, to impress and influence people every time you speak. You'll learn to express your ideas and the benefits of your product or service with clarity, precision, and laser-sharp focus. And once you do, you'll gain a competitive advantage. You will stand out like never before. You will reap the benefits. You will shine.

Lets's Get Started!

To really analyze your voice and make the necessary changes and improvements, you will need some way of recording yourself doing the exercises in this book. A simple cassette recorder is fine. Or you can use an answering machine or voicemail system.

I'd like to forewarn you about the first time you listen to your own voice on tape. Most people, to be honest, are shocked. They may even feel embarrassed or uncomfortable about the way they think they sound. I'll tell you why this happens.

You spend your entire life listening to your voice from inside your head. But the sound of the voice you hear in that head of yours is distorted by the bones of your skull. It's not your true sound.

Nevertheless, this is the voice you are used to, so when you hear your voice on tape, you reject it because it sounds strange. But remember this: the voice you hear on tape is the same voice others hear when they listen to you speak. And this is the voice you will have to work with. The only way you will ever change that voice into the one you want is by recording yourself for feedback.

You Must Remember This . . .

√ That most business relationships rely on the telephone and how you sound makes up 84 percent of the message you send. All the dress-for-success wardrobes in the world can't help you if you can't be seen.

√ That learning to manipulate the tone of your voice at will can improve people's instinctive reactions to you.

√ That the "first brain" of the people listening to you responds to vocal pitch, inflection, and tone. If anything in your voice seems threatening, boring, phony, or hostile, you might as well hang up because you're not going to convince your listener of anything.

√ That no one likes the sound of his own voice on a tape recorder, especially the first time around. But using a cassette recorder or an answering machine plays a vital role in your voice improvement. Make sure you have one handy as you read this book.

2

Banish Non-Words From Your Speech—Forever!

What are non-words? They are meaningless fillers that speckle our speech, distract from our message, drain our impact, and annoy our listener. I call them "verbal viruses" because they seem to be contagious and we pick them up without being aware of it.

The most common verbal viruses are "uhh," "ahh," and "um." But they also include "like," "you know," "well," "so," "okay?" "sort of" and other meaningless phrases we use to fill up the blank spaces between our thoughts.

When I give VoiceShaping® workshops for professional groups, someone inevitably comes up to me and says "You've got to help me do something about my teenager. She seems to have lost the ability to speak intelligently. Her entire vocabulary consists of about seven words: awesome, like, you know, way cool, not! and other such phrases."

If this sounds familiar to you, don't worry. Teens have been speaking their own language forever. They fall in love with fad words just as they fall in and out of love with the latest musical groups, fashions, and boy or girlfriend of the week. It's just a phase, and it, too, will pass.

What you should be concerned about, however, are any trite or overused phrases that YOU may be using, even inadvertently. One phrase that seems to have taken hold in my house lately is "whatever," as in "Would you like to go to a movie tonight?" "Whatever." Or, "You can put the book on the table, or whatever." To me, using "whatever" as a catch phrase makes the speaker sound as if he is shrugging off the rest of the conversation—it's as if he's given up or is too depressed to continue. There's also an element of rudeness in "whatever:" it expresses not only a verbal shrug, but also a distinct lack of interest in what someone else is saying.

Another curious misusage that keeps popping up is the substitution of the verb "to go" for the verb "to say." Does this sound familiar? "So I go to my boss, I need a raise, and he goes, no way, profits are down."

Using odd or meaningless phrases like these can cause the conversation of an intelligent adult to sound anything but intelligent. In fact, it brands the speaker as someone who is not very bright, whether or not this is true. I have heard these verbal viruses in the speech of lawyers, doctors, and other well-educated adults. They are jarring to the ear, inconsistent with a professional image, and demeaning to the speaker.

The biggest problem with verbal viruses is that they make us appear unsure, hesitant, and even incompetent. Nobody wants to be labeled with these descriptors, but non-words still creep insidiously into our speech. It is an unconscious habit—we don't even know how many times we use them until we hear ourselves on tape. I'll be telling you how to do this in the next chapter.

And as long as you are checking yourself for annoying vocal habits, be sure to check for irritating mouth sounds, as well. These include frequent smacking of the lips, and clicking or popping noises.

Inoculate Yourself Against Verbal Viruses

If non-words are your nemesis, you're in some pretty good company. Several years ago, then-Secretary of Defense Casper Weinberger held a televised press conference following a retaliatory air strike against Libya. It was a tense situation, and his appearance was a brief three minutes.

But in that short time there were 59 "umm"s and "ahh"s in Weinberger's speech. Millions were watching as he hemmed and hawed along, and Weinberger seemed hesitant and unsure of himself when he should have been making the American people feel confident that they could trust the military decision to act aggressively in this potentially explosive situation.

How do we stamp out these verbal viruses? The cure is simple. The most powerful way you can eliminate unwanted filler words and annoying mouth sounds is to replace them. And the best thing to replace them with is a pause. Whenever you catch yourself using a non-word, just stop talking for a moment and say nothing. Now, I have to warn you—the first few times you do this, it will probably feel as though there is an enormous, scary, canyon-sized gap of silence while you wait. But I promise you the listener will scarcely notice.

As you practice pausing between thoughts, you will become more and more comfortable in the gap. And you will also discover something interesting: A pause helps draw the audience in and captures their interest. Studies show that you can pause for as long as four seconds, right in the middle of a sentence, and it will seem perfectly natural to those listening to you.

Start practicing your pauses today. Before long, you will discover how wonderful silence can be. It can help you gather your thoughts while giving the listener time to reflect on what you have just said. More importantly, the power of the pause adds drama and impact to your message, while making you seem more confident, poised, and in-control.

Here's more proof of the power of the pause. If you are ever called upon to speak in front of a noisy crowd, don't try to shout above the din. Just stand at the front of the room and say nothing. The room will gradually fall silent and within minutes you will notice that all eyes are on you, eager to hear what you have to say. The sound of silence is the most eloquent sound in the world.

Broadcaster's Tip
Silence is golden

A pause can be a powerful thing. Strategically placed pauses draw the listener in, adding power and impact to your message.

While silence is, indeed, golden, here are three other tools to use to break the non-word habit.

• Send yourself copies of the voicemail messages you leave for others. Listen to them at the end of the day and note whether or not any unwanted fillers crept into your message.

• Enlist the help of your spouse or a friend. Explain what you are trying to do, and invent a code word he or she can use every time you use a filler word.

• When you feel you are about to use a non-word, take a breath, hold it for a moment, and then begin to speak. The focus on your breathing will occupy your mind, keep you calm and centered, and make the silence between the words seem much less scary.

Breathing Lessons

One of the biggest concerns among people seeking to improve their voices is breathing. Most people believe that the way to achieve rich, resonant speaking tones is by doing some sort of special breathing exercises. They think that to project the voice or improve vocal tone they have to pump strenuously or push from the diaphragm. They are convinced that the breath alone must carry the voice.

Nothing could be further from the truth. Let me debunk some major myths about breathing and the voice.

If breath alone were the only means we had to project the voice, a stage actor who wanted to be heard in the last row of the theatre would have to blow eight times harder than the worst hurricane. Even Orson Welles couldn't have managed this, and anyway it would blow the theatre and the audience to bits. The sound of your voice is amplified and strengthened by resonance and wave reflection, not by breath. Too much breath disperses the sound waves and destroys resonance. The result? A weak, breathy sound that can scarcely be heard and that can injure the vocal chords.

The vocal sound stream and breathing are two completely different things. To achieve good speaking tone, you need an almost infinitesimal amount of breath. Think of it as blowing across a bottle or into a flute. If you blow too much, you get little or no sound at all. In fact, if you are aware of your breath at all while speaking, or if you try to control it in any way, you are overdoing it. So how do you breathe for good speaking? Just breathe naturally.

For many people, this is easier said than done, because as we grow older we tend to restrict our breath as a way of controlling our emotions. Consider this: most little children have no problem expressing themselves and being heard. And most little children breathe naturally.

It isn't until early adolescence that we start to clam up and clamp down on the flood of emotions we feel on entering adulthood. We become sullen and moody and frequently communicate with adults in tight little sentences. To free the voice, we need to regain the relaxed and unobstructed breathing of our early childhood.

You can't breathe naturally if you are under physical or emotional stress, if you are not physically fit, or if you have poor posture. When speaking on the phone to a friend, can't you tell almost immediately if that person is tired or depressed or sick? Haven't you noticed the difference in talking to someone who is slumped on the couch or is standing up straight? So deep breathing exercises are important for good speech, not because they affect the power of the voice, but because they help reduce stress and keep us centered and relaxed. And believe me, the stronger and healthier you feel, the better you will sound. Yet very few people breathe correctly while standing upright or sitting normally in a chair, because they have gotten used to holding themselves in a way that restricts the body from breathing naturally.

Ready, Set, . . . Breathe

Fortunately, it is very easy to experience what natural breathing feels like. Try this exercise:

- Stand in front of a full-length mirror. Relax.

- Let your arms hang loosely at your sides and do not think about breathing. In a moment, natural breathing will take over.

Observe your body while breathing naturally.

•   Place one hand on your abdomen and the other on your chest. Note that as you breathe naturally, your upper chest is relaxed, moving only slightly, while your abdomen moves gently in and out.

What's happening inside your body while you are observing yourself in the mirror? Your diaphragm, the strong muscle located below the bottom of the rib cage, beneath the abdominal wall, is pushing out the abdominal wall as you inhale, so the rib cage can expand, making room for your lungs to fill with air. As the diaphragm relaxes, and you exhale, air flows up and out of the body through the nose. We use this exhaled breath stream to form sound. In a healthy person, there is always enough exhaled breath to allow us to speak.

Here are three factors that interfere with natural breathing and diminish our resonance and speaking power.

1   **Muscle tension.**
    Tense muscles always affect the breathing and the quality of the voice, especially if there is tension in the abdomen, shoulders, and neck.

2   **Habitual breathing patterns.**
    Breathing patterns you learned by imitating family members as a child.

3   **Your ability to feel and express emotions.**
    People who know you can tell how you feel just by the way you say hello.

When feelings are unexpressed or something is troubling us, our breathing quickly loses its natural quality. It becomes jagged, shallow, uneven. It's instinctive to want to hold your breath when faced with fear or overwhelming emotion. Animals do this so they can listen for danger without being distracted by the sound of their own breathing. In humans, this instinct is a carryover from our primitive ancestors. Today, by reminding ourselves to breathe naturally when feeling pressured, we can calm ourselves down, release our voices, and regain our composure.

Try the following exercise to help you speak more smoothly.

• Record yourself reading aloud from a newspaper or magazine. At the end of each thought, or where there is a comma or semicolon, take a little breath. Take another full breath at the end of the sentence.

• Marking up the copy you are reading may help. At commas or semicolons, use a slash mark (\). For a full breath at the end of the sentence, use a double slash (\\). If the sentence is long and wordy, you may want to pause for your small breath at the end of each thought.

Exercises

According to speech pathologist Dr. Lillian Glass, the three most common breathing problems are these:

1   Taking in too much air, filling up the upper chest, and not using the diaphragm to speak.

2   Taking in too many little breaths.

3   Exhaling all the air and speaking on virtually no air.

To breathe properly, you should feel as though your waistline is expanding, not your upper chest. To practice, lie down in a comfortable spot. Place one hand on your upper chest and the other at your waistline. Slowly and gently, breathe in through your mouth to the count of three. Your chest should be still and your waistline should expand. Hold for a count of three. Now, breathe out through your mouth for a count of six. Your abdomen should contract and your chest should remain still. Repeat four times. If you feel light-headed, slow down. That means you went too fast and are beginning to hyperventilate. Now sit up and try the exercise again. This exercise is also a good one for relaxation, so try it whenever you feel stressed.

Here's another breathing exercise for stress reduction. (You can do this one sitting or standing.) Make a fist and place it lightly against your abdomen. Gently breathe in through your mouth for a count of three. Feel your abdomen expand beneath your fist. Hold for three. Now relax your jaw and let your tongue fall to the bottom of your mouth, making sure the back of your tongue is relaxed and down and your throat is open—as if you were about to yawn. Now exhale for a count of six—as you do this, make your lowest, deepest sound. Try it again. Feel the sound open the back of your throat and resonate deep in your abdomen (where your fist is resting.) Do this exercise four times.

Your voice may not sound as you want it to in professional speaking situations because the emotional energy you feel at these highly charged times causes you to tense up and restricts your breathing. For many of us, the first muscles to tighten are those in the middle of the body. Your breathing becomes shallow, forced up into the chest and throat. The result is a voice that sounds weak, shaky, and insecure.

Communications consultant Dr. Joan Kenley says we can avoid this problem by focusing our breathing on the group of muscles we cough with in the lower torso. You can try this exercise lying down or sitting up

Place one hand on your abdomen just below your navel. Cough deeply so you can feel the group of muscles I am talking about. If you imagine that your breath is centered here, you will feel as though your voice is "grounded." Now breathe in gently through your mouth and let the breath lift the cough muscle area just below your navel. Your upper chest should barely move as you inhale. Make no extra effort to move the middle of your torso—just let it expand naturally as you inhale. As you exhale, let the cough muscle fall back toward your spine as it moves a column of air up and out of your body. Practice this exercise several times until it becomes second nature. Then practice it daily. By letting the strength of your lower body support your breath, the beauty and resonance of your voice will improve dramatically.

Broadcaster's Tip
Mark your copy

When I am in the recording studio doing voice-overs, I will often mark my script with a " ^ " to indicate a breathing point. It helps my delivery. I also use " ↑ " to indicate upward inflection, " ↓ " to indicate downward inflection and " → " to remind me to link two ideas.

You Must Remember This . . .

√   Non-words are the meaningless fillers in our speech that distract and annoy the listener and drain impact from our message.

√   The first step in curing the non-word habit is to identify the enemy. Record yourself and count how many fillers you used .

√   That once you become aware of your most-used non-words, consciously replace them with a pause.

√   You can control the non-word habit by monitoring the voicemail messages you leave for others; by getting your spouse or a friend to say "bingo" or other code word every time you use a non-word; and by simply pausing when you feel a non-word coming on.

√   That the four things that interfere with natural breathing are poor posture, tense muscles, breathing habits, and the ability to express emotion.

√   That breathing exercises can relax us and improve our mental state, which in itself alone, improves the sound of the voice.

3

Evaluate Your Voice

If you don't like hearing your voice on an answering machine or tape recorder, you might be feeling a little nervous about the voice evaluation coming up.

As I mentioned in Chapter 1, the voice you hear when you speak is not your true voice. That's because the sound of your voice inside your head is distorted by the bones of your skull. Your true voice, the voice other people hear when you speak, is the voice you hear when you listen to yourself on tape. And because you are not used to it, you will probably think your voice sounds too nasal, too high or too low. Whatever reaction you have will probably be negative.

Once we have evaluated your voice, we can determine whether you are right about your self-criticism, or whether you are being overly severe on yourself. But it's important to remember this: there is a huge difference between the way we think we sound and the way others hear us.

This is because of a phenomenon known as disparity, which in this case is defined as the gap between how we feel about the way we come across versus what others are thinking and feeling about us. Learning to deal with this particular definition of disparity is critical if you want to become a more effective, powerful communicator.

Communications expert Bert Decker says once we fully grasp

that the way we feel is not the way we come across, we gain the courage and confidence to deliver livelier, more energetic presentations, revealing more of our true selves to others.

In my own work behind the microphone and in my work training others, I've found that hearing oneself on tape is the best way to close the disparity gap. Without audio feedback, we are clueless about the way we really sound to others and we cannot be objective about our own vocal strengths and areas that may need some improvement.

If we have any opinion at all about our own voice, it tends to be overwhelmingly negative. In fact, most people get fixated on what's wrong with their voices and completely ignore what's right. Most people are brutally hard on themselves. And this is not at all conducive to growth and development.

To get the results you want, you need to learn to listen to your voice with an objective ear; as if you were listening to the voice of another person—someone you cared about and really wanted to help. Remember, the key to all effective and persuasive communication is this: The way we feel is not the way we come across. Make a sign for your desk if you need to, but don't forget these very important words.

How To Evaluate Your Voice

Evaluating your voice is a four step process. First, you will record your voice (on tape or on voicemail) in two different kinds of speaking situations: ad-libbing, or talking "off-the-cuff," and then reading from the script you will find at the end of this chapter. In Step 2, you will listen to the tape and evaluate what you hear on the forms provided. In Step 3, you will have a few supportive friends and colleagues listen and evaluate your voice. And in Step 4, you will compare and contrast your self-evaluation with those of your associates.

This feedback process is extremely valuable. Here are the results you can expect: You will immediately get to see disparity at work in your own life as you find out exactly how big a gap exists between the way you think you sound and the way others hear you; you will also begin to see if you are being too hard on yourself. Or maybe you will discover there are some facets of your "spoken image" that need work. Remember, knowledge is power—and self-knowledge is the most powerful knowledge of all.

Broadcaster's Tip
Aircheck yourself

An aircheck is a tape made of an actual broadcast for later review by an on-air personality and their program director. An aircheck is an essential feedback tool for growth and improvement. Think of yourself as "on the air" when you make your daily business calls. Aircheck yourself once each month by taping a days worth of calls. Listen to the tape objectively to analyze your effectiveness.

Set Yourself Up—To Succeed

First, write down the names of at least two or three supportive friends or colleagues who would be willing to give you constructive feedback on your voice and communication skills. You can assure them that this should not take more than 10 or 15 minutes of their time.

The people I choose to help me evaluate my voice are:

1 _____

2 _____

3 _____

You may photocopy this form for future use

Second, gather your materials: note pad and pencil, tape recorder or voicemail, script provided at the end of the chapter.

Third, make a photocopy of the evaluation sheet for each colleague who will be evaluating your voice.

Ready, Set . . . Talk!

First, we will do the speech that you will ad-lib. Before you begin, make a few notes to yourself to keep from drawing a blank as you speak. Don't worry about making a mistake or stumbling—I just want you to speak spontaneously for about a minute. What will you talk about? Tell me about yourself—your name, where you were born, how old you are, something about your family. What do you look like? Where did you go to school? Do you live in an apartment or a house? How many rooms? What does it look like? Do you like it? Tell me what you do for a living—describe a typical work day or simply tell me about your dreams and your vision for your future.

When you have finished, set the tape aside or save the message on your voicemail.

Now look at the evaluation script on page 26. You may want to practice reading it aloud a couple of times before actually recording it. Reading silently will not get the mind and the mouth working together—it is important to practice aloud.

All right, that's enough practice—turn the page and read me that speech.

Check As Many As Apply

After listening to yourself speaking spontaneously and reading from a script, how do you feel about the quality of your voice? Look at the lists on pages 27 and 28. One is for things you like about your voice, the other is things you may want to improve. Be sure to listen to your tape several times to get a real handle on how you sound.

On page 27 you'll find the "speaking strengths" list.

On page 28 you'll find the "needs improvement" list.

Check as many of these descriptors as you feel apply to your voice in the two readings.

Read this script into a tape recorder

Voice Evaluation Script

Many people think that communicating effectively is merely a matter of finding and using the right magic words. They believe that using certain words in the right order, will get them the results they want.

Unfortunately, these people are living in a dream world. Scientific research tells us that attempting to persuade by words alone is about as effective as trying to chop down a tree with a Swiss Army knife.

In a study conducted at UCLA, Dr. Albert Mehrabian found that when verbal, vocal and visual signals are inconsistent, content counts for a mere seven percent of the overall message. Most of our message—about 55 percent—is sent by facial expressions and body language; but 38 percent depends on the quality of our voices—pitch, tone, volume, and inflection.

The implications of this are shocking. If anything about your voice is flat or distracting, annoying or boring, you could be reducing your effectiveness by 38 percent!

Here is the "speaking strengths" list

☐   warm   ☐   interesting
☐   passionate   ☐   convincing
☐   enthusiastic   ☐   clear speech
☐   articulate   ☐   professional
☐   well paced   ☐   commanding
☐   pleasant tone   ☐   trustworthy

If you have other adjectives you would like to apply to your voice, jot them down:

_____

_____

_____

_____

_____

_____

_____

_____

_____

_____

You may photocopy this form for future use

Here is the "needs improvement" list

☐ too fast   ☐ too slow
☐ singsong   ☐ monotone
☐ sounds tired   ☐ unpleasant tone
☐ hyper   ☐ threatening
☐ breathy   ☐ nasal
☐ mumbles   ☐ overly-precise
☐ too loud   ☐ too-soft
☐ tentative   ☐ too high-pitched
☐ strong accent/regionalism
☐ too many "verbal viruses

That's my list, but if I've left anything out, jot it down.
Make some notes on how you feel about your voice.

_____

_____

_____

_____

_____

_____

You may photocopy this form for future use

Reactions

You have just given yourself a lot of feedback. You will notice that some of the feedback relates to tone and speaking style, while some of it relates to articulation and pronunciation. How do you feel about what you just heard and the evaluation you gave yourself? Do you think you sounded pretty good? Or do you feel frustrated, embarrassed, surprised?

Broadcaster's Tip
Work on improving only one thing at a time

As you tape yourself for feedback, you might feel overwhelmed. Make a list of things you wish to change about your voice and work on them one by one. Trying to tackle too many things at once will only depress you. For example, don't try to work on pacing if you are concentrating on improving your articulation. Take as long as you need to master one skill before moving on to the next.

Speaking Of Pronunciation . . .

Here is my Top 10 list of common pronunciation mistakes that can make you sound uneducated and less intelligent than you really are. How many of these apply to you?

1   **Get the "L" in there.**
        Do you say "awready" and "awright" instead of "aLready" and "aLL right"?

2   **"T" and "D" are <u>not</u> interchangeable.**
        Do you say "qualiDy" instead of "qualiTy"? Or

"diTn't" for "diDn't"? "SevenDY" instead of
"sevenTy"?

3   **The murderous switcheroo.**
Substituting AXE for ASK. Think about it: "I
will AXE him if he wants to come." With an
invitation like that, he probably will decline.

4   **The "R" vs. "OUR" syndrome.**
Self-explanatory—do you say "R" house, when
you mean "OUR" house?

5   **Probable cause.**
Do you shorten "PROBABLY" to "PROBLY"
or "PROLLY?" Listen to yourself carefully.

6   **"I" and "E" confusion**
Lots of Americans make "E" and "I" interchangeable when they speak. For instance,
"Do you have a pIn I can write with?" Fat
chance.

7   **The THEM horror story.**
Do you say "thUm" instead of "thEm"? You're
not alone, but try to avoid it.

8   **Keep the "FUR" on the animals!**
Do you substitute "FUR" for "FOR?" When
calling someone to the phone, do you say "It's
FUR you?"

9   **Are you abusing poor little "TO?"**
Too many people say "TUH" instead of "TO."
Do these examples sound familiar? "I'm going
TUHDAY" instead of "TODAY." Or how
about "I'm going TUH the store." When you

count you don't say one, TUH, three, do you?
I hope not. Remember—TO, TWO, and TOO
are all pronounced the same way.

10   **Getting the jist of it.**
The word is "jUst" not "jIst." Try to remember
"justice."

Vowels, Consonants, And Dictionaries

Our language consists of vowels and consonants. The way you
handle those vowels and consonants affects the color and clarity of your
speech. Vowels add color and music to speech, consonants add clarity.
For example, if you took all the consonants from the sentence "The
dog sat down," you would end up with the letters e, o, a , and o. And
you would have a tough time figuring out what this sentence meant. But
if you took away the vowels, the consonants would provide enough
clarity for you to guess the meaning—th dg st dwn.

You can learn much about word pronunciation by studying any
good dictionary. Let's take the word "abdicate." If you look it up in
your dictionary, you will notice that in parentheses next to the word
there is a phonetic spelling, which also acts as a guide to pronunciation.

$$\breve{} \quad \bar{} \quad \bar{}$$
ab'di-kat'

Notice that there are some markings over the "A"s and the "C" has
been replaced by a "K", so you know how to pronounce that "C."
What do those markings over the "A"s mean? If you look in your
dictionary's pronunciation guide, it will explain those markings. In my
largest dictionary, the American Heritage Dictionary of the English
Language, running across the bottom of the page under a rule are
explanations of these marks, which are called diacritical marks. The
little half circle over the first "A" means it is a "short a" pronounced as in

the word "pat." The straight line over the second "A" indicates it is a "long a" to be pronounced as in the word "cake." Once you become familiar with diacritical marks, you will never have to wonder how a word is pronounced.

Accents - Charming Or Annoying?

In a country as large and culturally diverse as the United States, it is only natural that the vowels and consonants of American English will have many different pronunciations, depending on which part of the country you are from, your ethnic background, and the dialects and accents of the people around you when you were growing up.

Regional, ethnic, and foreign accents add color, flavor, and music to the sound of America. But they can also evoke certain stereotypical judgments in the mind of the listener, and this can affect the way you and your message are perceived.

Complete elimination of a foreign or regional accent can take months of intensive work with a private speech and diction coach. Coaches can usually be found through the drama department of your local university. Only you can decide whether it is worth your time and money to invest in a coach.

The Four Learning Stages

There are four stages of learning that everyone must go through to learn a new skill or master self-improvement.

1   The first stage is "unconscious incompetence," or what I call the clueless stage. That is where you don't know what you don't know—and it's where you were before you started working with this book.

2   The second stage is "conscious incompetence."
That is where you know what you don't know, and
you probably don't like not knowing it. As you
become conscious of your speech, it is rather like
opening Pandora's Box. You become painfully
conscious of every "um," every missed consonant,
every slur. You feel as though you are the most
inarticulate person on the planet. But take heart—
to the people around you, you sound the way you
always have. They will start noticing, however, in a
few weeks when you've taken the steps necessary
to improve your voice.

3   The third learning stage is more comfortable. It's
called "conscious competence." Here you notice
your improvement. People begin to complement
you on the sound of your voice. You still have to
think about what you are doing, but you are actually
beginning to master the skill.

4   The fourth and final learning stage is "unconscious
competence." It is at this stage that the skill you
have been trying to acquire becomes second nature
to you—so fully integrated into your mind that you
don't even need to think about it.

By completing your voice evaluation, you have just entered into
stage 1, the state of "conscious incompetence." I know it's uncomfortable, but unfortunately it is impossible to learn anything without passing
through this stage—this is the stage where the most growth and self-
discovery occur. It also requires that you suspend self-judgement and
not take yourself too seriously—otherwise, you risk giving up or giving
in to defeat. And this would be a waste of your time and your talent
and your potential. Stick with it.

Broadcaster's Tip
**Seek professional help with
your diction**

Even though you may not be a
broadcaster, the quality of your
voice is just as important to your professional
success. If you suffer from articulation problems,
speech impediments or a distracting accent, do
as the broadcasters do and get help from a
competent speech pathologist or coach.

The Importance Of Consensus

In the next few days, be sure that your friends or colleagues
listen to and evaluate your voice. You need to find out as soon as
possible which of your self-evaluations were right, and where you were
being too hard on yourself.

In going over the evaluation sheets, look first for areas of
consensus—points that everyone agrees on are areas that need improvement. These are the areas you should focus on first for greatest
impact. And it is safe to assume that unless your self-criticism is
corroborated by at least one person, it is not valid. It's rare not to see
any consensus among the evaluations. If, by some chance, it does
happen, have your tape evaluated by a few more people until consensus
is reached.

At the end of the evaluation process, you will be able to measure the disparity gap between the way you feel about how you sound
and the way you come across to others. And this is exactly the kind of
information you need to make a quantum leap in improving your powers
of persuasion and self-expression.

You Must Remember This . . .

√   That there is a huge difference between the way we perceive ourselves and the way others perceive us. This is called disparity.

√   That working with your voice on tape and getting constructive feedback from others is the best way to bridge the gap between the way we think we sound and the way we really do sound.

√   That a dialect or regional accent can cause people to make unfair judgments about you and your products or services. Working to bring your speech close to standard American English can help reduce or eliminate this effect.

√   There are four stages of learning that everyone must go through in order to learn a new skill or master self-improvement. They are uncon scious incompetence, conscious incompetence, conscious competence, and unconscious competence.

√   Learning to hear yourself as others hear you takes patience and courage. But it is the only way to make rapid and powerful changes in the way you speak.

4

Sound Like You Mean Business . . . Even When You Feel Like A Wimp Inside

Ralph Waldo Emerson once said: "Nothing great was ever achieved without enthusiasm."

You can't become an enthusiastic speaker if you don't communicate with every fiber of your being. This is what we will be working on in this chapter.

Many people think that communicating is an activity centered in the mouth and throat; however, after more than 20 years as a professional broadcaster, I have discovered that it takes much more than that to be the kind of persuasive, concise, and articulate speaker you want to be.

Some people have the idea that to communicate powerfully and effectively, you must learn a host of complicated techniques and skills. The task seems daunting—as if you were a musician about to prepare for a virtuoso performance or an athlete training for the Olympics. Nothing could be further from the truth.

Voice-over artists are experts at changing the sound of their voice on cue. Directors often ask us to read the same script in many different ways: authoritative, warm, energetic, mellow. But whatever we do, it must sound believable and sincere. To accomplish this feat, I use a three-step method. I have discovered that to express yourself fully and congruently you merely need to access the proper emotional state. You do this by giving yourself cues which are auditory (heard), kinesthetic (felt), and visual (seen).

My three-step method

I have found that every tone of voice has a corresponding:

1	Key word-auditory cue
2	Mental image-visual cue
3	Body language-kinesthetic cue

Key Word: Your auditory cue

Using a single word, name the overriding feeling you'd like to convey in your presentation. For an authoritative tone of voice choose a dynamic, active word such as "power," "win," "strong," "go" or "yes" (my favorite). Say this word over and over aloud with gusto!

Mental Image: Your visual cue

As you say your authoritative key word out loud a movie will begin to form in your mind. Keep saying your key word over and over making the image in your mind clear and bright. For an authoritative tone of voice some people see themselves as a coach, an executive or a military officer. Find the image that works for you. But notice all the cinematic details, the colors, the set design, the supporting players.

Body Language: Your kinesthetic cue

The fastest way to change the sound of your voice is to change your physiology. Make your body language BIG. To sound more authoritative, stand up! Make sure your posture is erect, your hand gestures strong, and your gaze firm. When speaking on the phone, don't let your eyes wander. If you are alone in the room, fix your gaze on the eyes of a person in a photograph on your desk or in a magazine.

This technique may sound a little strange, but it really works!

As children, we were all master communicators. Think of any three-year-old you know and you will agree she has absolutely no trouble expressing herself. Your task is to recover some of the youthful spontaneity and expressiveness lost over the years and put it to use. My task is to help you do it quickly and efficiently through the series of exercises that follow.

Imagine a time in the past when words flowed effortlessly. You felt the rapt attention of the listener. You connected. You were comfortable with the subject matter. You felt passionate about what you were saying. You were completely relaxed and at ease, without the slightest trace of self-consciousness.

In this state, you communicated with your entire body: your eyes shone, your hands were expressive, your face lit up. And you probably made a positive and favorable impression on your audience.

Psychologists use a term called "affect" to describe our emotions and moods. They measure "affect" on a scale from zero to 100. Zero is the zombie state—completely devoid of emotional energy, lifeless, colorless, flat. To be at 100 percent "affect" is to express yourself with so much energy and enthusiasm that you are practically bouncing off the walls, going full throttle, way over the top. It's the difference between "Night of the Living Dead" and Roger Rabbit.

Where are you on the "affect" scale? Children tend to be closer to Roger Rabbit. Once we were all this way, but as we grow up our natural exuberance is deadened. At school and at home we are taught to be quiet. To be seen and not heard. As a result, we learn to repress our enthusiasm. This can cause a once-joyful and expressive child to sound like Henry Kissinger by the time he reaches the age of 25.

Our goal as effective communicators is to unlock our natural energy. Not to sound like maniacs, but to express ourselves freely and let our emotions flow through our voices as mood and circumstance dictate. To be a truly effective communicator, you must project passion and enthusiasm for your subject. Energy attracts attention; it draws the listener in. But when we are nervous our natural flow of energy is blocked and the audience tends to tune us out. In the exercises that follow, you'll learn techniques to help you project the energy necessary for effective communication, even when your natural enthusiasm is dampened by nerves.

Body Language

In training hundreds of people to become professional voice-over artists, I have discovered that the quickest and easiest way to change the sound of your voice is to do something different with your body.

When you think of using your body while you speak, you may feel embarrassed, uncomfortable, afraid of looking foolish. But remember the disparity principle: The way we feel is not necessarily the way we come across.

Let's explore some easy ways you can use your body to become a more energetic, natural communicator. Your posture, your gestures, your facial expressions all have an enormous and immediate impact on the way you sound. For example, if you habitually slump in your chair while talking on the phone, I guarantee that the tone of your voice is going to sound slumped and the people you call may find it hard to concentrate on what you are saying. Why? Because there is no energy in your voice to capture their interest. Powerful, persuasive communicators always use their bodies to express themselves, consciously or not. They speak with their hands. Their eyes sparkle. Their faces express every emotion. Their body language is fluid and alive.

Making Faces

One of the fastest ways I have found to make the voice more expressive is to make the face more expressive. When it comes to facial expressions, there are three distinct groups of people. The first group is naturally expressive: they smile easily and often. Their facial expressions and tone of voice are generally positive, expressive and upbeat; they are terrible at poker because everything shows on their faces.

The second group is the neutral group. Their facial expressions shift from serious to happy depending on their moods. And the third group is what I call the secret smilers. You know you are a secret smiler if people frequently ask you what is wrong even when you feel as though you are smiling and happy inside. Secret smilers tend to look intense and may scowl when they are concentrating.

If you are in the neutral or secret smiler group, your voice may tend to flatten and sound monotonous when you have a lot on your mind. To add more life to your voice, pay close attention to the following exercises. They will help increase your facial flexibility and your range of facial expression. And by so doing, you will gain added flexibility and expression in your voice.

For the following exercises, you will need a mirror and a television set.

Facial Flexibility Exercise #1

1   Turn on the TV, but not the sound.

2   Channel surf until you find a movie, drama, or sitcom.

3 Watch for a few minutes and notice the reaction shots (a reaction shot is a close-up of an actor when he is reacting to another's speech, but not speaking any lines himself).

4 Identify the emotion the actor is trying to convey. If he's any good, it should be crystal clear.

Facial Flexibility Exercise #2

1 With your mirror handy, turn on a TV news show. (CNN has news 24 hours a day.)

2 Keeping your face as relaxed and neutral as possible, watch two or three stories. Turn off the TV.

3 Looking in your hand mirror, pretend that you are mute and have to express the feeling of each story to an imaginary third person. Do this with your facial expressions only. If there is someone around, ask him to identify what emotions you are trying to express.

Facial Flexibility Exercise #3

This is a great exercise if you discovered in your voice evaluation that you needed to sound warmer and friendlier. To put a smile in your voice, all you have to do is put a smile on your face while you talk.

1 Stand in front of a mirror and think of a time when you were extremely happy. Relive the moment. Watch your face and keep thinking of the moment until you can actually see the joy on your face. Study how your face moves when you feel this emotion.

2   Close your eyes. Try to remember the tension and feeling in your facial muscles. Now relax your face into a neutral expression. Without thinking of the happy time, see if you can re-create a joyful expression just by using muscle memory alone.

3   Try this exercise again, using the emotions of sadness and anger. See how close you can come to creating a sad or angry look on cue.

4   Now set up your tape recorder and prepare to record. Keeping your hand mirror close by, recreate your happy look as you did before. When you are beaming with joy, record the following sentence while looking in the mirror:

Today I ate lunch with Bill and Sally. We all had burgers and fries.

(Do not play the tape back yet.)

5   Now recreate the sad look. While looking in the mirror, record the same sentence. If your face lapses into a neutral expression, stop and re-focus until the sad look comes back. (Do not play the tape back yet.)

6   Now get furious. Still holding the mirror, record the same sentence. Turn off the tape recorder. Relax for a minute (all that emoting can be strenuous stuff.) Now listen to what you have just recorded. The sentence is emotionally neutral, but can you hear how much expression you can get in your voice just

by changing the expression on your face?

Facial Flexibility Exercise #4

Have you ever had a telephone conversation with someone who is distracted? It feels as though you are talking to a wall. I call this having a blank stare in the voice. And any of us can get these blank stares in our voices when we have to talk while preoccupied. This exercise will get the stare out of your voice, make you stay focused, and make contact in person or over the phone.

1   If you are in a face-to-face situation, look the other person in the eye and talk. If you are on the phone, imagine the person's face as you see it in your mind's eye. Keep your eyes focused and your face relaxed. This will create an empathetic sound in your voice.

Some telephone sales pros keep a picture of a loved one on their desks. Then they speak to the picture as they talk to their prospect. Other highly imaginative sales reps picture that the person to whom they are speaking has shrunk and is sitting right there on the telephone receiver.

Broadcaster's Tip
Speak to just one person

When I was doing radio work, I used to mentally superimpose the face of a close friend right over the microphone. And even though I was speaking to hundreds of thousands of people, in my mind I was having an intimate conversation with just one person that I knew and loved.

Your Mother Was Right . . . Posture Counts

If you discovered in your voice evaluation that you sound low-key or depressed and you would like to inject more energy and enthusiasm into your voice, take a look at your posture.

Speaking while hunched or slumped over will tend to pull the energy out of your voice. If you do a lot of work over the telephone, take a look at your desk chair. It should be one that allows you to sit up straight and provides proper back support.

Make sure your computer monitor is properly positioned so you are looking straight at it. If you have to drop or lower your jaw to see the screen while speaking on the phone, the tension in your neck will prevent you from sounding your best.

If bad posture is a chronic problem, try this classic posture exercise. Find a bare wall (preferably with no base molding). Stand against this wall, heels and shoulders touching it. Now press the small of your back against the wall—at least as much as you can. If you can get your shoulders, the small of your back, and your heels touching the wall, you will be absolutely straight. And if you practice this every day, you will notice the improvement in your stance.

Here's another one: Hang a string down the center of a full-length mirror. Facing the mirror, align yourself so that your body is bisected by the string. Your feet will be directly under your armpits. Keep your knees relaxed. Bring your head, shoulders and hips into alignment so your body is evenly distributed on both sides of the string. Take a deep breath. This is what being physically centered feels like.

If you are called on to speak, think of getting into a tennis stance. Your energy should be directed forward to the balls of your feet, weight evenly distributed, knees flexible. This will help you feel energized, grounded, and in control. And your voice will reflect that.

You can bet that people who spend a lot of time addressing others make use of all these tips. When I watched the O.J. Simpson trial I noticed that defense attorney Johnny Cochran frequently leaned forward toward the jury. This body posture gave him energy and made it seem as though he were speaking to us as a friend or confidante, one-to-one. It did much to enhance his credibility and I am convinced Cochran's strong speaking skills had a significant effect on the outcome of the trial.

Hands Up!

Another part of your body that is vitally important for your speech is your hands. In my work training professional speakers I have noticed that whenever hands hang lifelessly or flutter, the person's voice sounds lifeless and devoid of energy. When hands hang by the side, it is as though energy is draining out of the fingertips.

Recently I was invited to speak on VoiceShaping® to a group of attorneys. After my presentation, a woman said to me that she felt she had a problem projecting her voice. Whenever she spoke in court, the court reporters complained they could not hear her. In passing, she mentioned that she was of Italian descent. The Italians are a wonderfully expressive, vibrant people. And they use their hands freely when they speak. When this woman became a lawyer, she felt she had to adopt a more sedate and conservative image. She forced herself to stop using her hands, because she did not think it fit the image of how a lawyer should act.

But in the process, she stifled her natural energy and enthusiasm. And because projection rides on energy, no one could hear what she was saying. I encouraged her to go back to using her hands and being her natural self. I assured her there was no way anyone could perceive this charming, poised woman as outrageous or inappropriate.

I will give you the same advice: If you want to sound more enthusiastic, gesture freely and keep your hands above your waist. It may surprise you to know that gesturing works equally well if you are on the phone. If I am holding the receiver in one hand, I use the other hand for gesturing. For maximum hands-free movement, I strongly recommend a headset. Another benefit of the headset is that it helps release tension in the neck and jaw, because you will not be tempted to hold the receiver between your ear and your shoulder as you speak. And as I mentioned earlier, a relaxed neck and jaw are essentials for a good vocal sound.

If you really need to sound "on" during an important phone call, try speaking standing up. Many pros have cordless headsets or long cords that allow them to walk around their offices using the same posture and gestures they would use in front of an audience.

The important thing to remember is not to adapt your essential self, the natural communicator within, to different audiences or speaking situations. Your goal is to get yourself to communicate as naturally and comfortably over the phone or in front of a crowd as you do sitting in your living room talking to a friend. You should communicate the same way to a TV camera or an audience of thousands as you would to that friend. No virtuoso performance needed.

Broadcaster's Tip
Create your own style

"You'll never be your best doing it someone else's way"

~Rush Limbaugh

You Must Remember This . . .

√ That to be an effective communicator, you must use your entire body, not just your vocal chords. We are born with everything we need to be enthusiastic communicators, but spontaneity declines as we get older.

√ That improving your posture will have an immediate and positive effect on the sound of your voice.

√ That putting a smile on your face will put a smile in your voice.

√ That to avoid a "blank stare" in your voice when you are preoccupied, keep your eyes focused and your face relaxed while you are on the phone.

√ That using your hands and gesturing freely adds color and energy to your speech.

√ That effective communication does not require a virtuoso performance. When speaking to one or one thousand, you should speak to your audience the way you would to your best friend.

5

Use The Power Of Your Mind To Shape Your Voice

Sit back for a moment and imagine a plane flying over New York City. As this plane flies over the Empire State building, the pilot pulls a lever and the doors of the cargo bay open, releasing an enormous, ripe, red strawberry that plummets through the air and lands right on top of King Kong's stomping grounds. Yes, a giant strawberry has just impaled itself on the pointy spire of the Empire State building. Look at that red juice dripping down the side of the building, oozing to the pavement below.

Did you see that? Of course you did. I just gave you an experience that would have taken Hollywood months and millions to create. Yet I did it in a second without spending a cent. I was the director, but you were the cinematographer, the set director, the actor. You were also the audience in this theatre—the theatre of the mind.

As you become a master communicator, you, too can become an expert director in the theatre of the mind and turn what was once a boring, mundane phone call or presentation into a cinematic experience. You can make your product and yourself seem more interesting, larger than life, and richer in detail than before. The beauty of this is that once you have mastered the technique, it doesn't matter how old you are, what you look like, what you are wearing, or how you feel. The voice can soar. It can project beauty, grace, power, and confidence. Remember the study where facially deformed people were perceived as more attractive when they had lovely voices? If properly cared for, the voice can be almost ageless. Mellowed by time, but not ravaged.

In *Psychocybernetics*, the ground-breaking book about the body/mind connection, Maxwell Maltz wrote: "The mind cannot tell the difference between an actual experience and one vividly imagined."

Of course, our rational minds can tell the difference, but the powerful, primitive part of our brains cannot distinguish reality from fantasy. That's why watching a horror movie can produce the symptoms of fear or terror: weak knees, damp palms, shallow breathing, rapid heartbeat. This is the power of visualization. Consider the following true story:

A golfer who had not set foot on a course for seven years improved his game by more than 20 strokes just by playing golf in his mind during the seven-year hiatus. The golfer was a soldier who was a prisoner of war in Vietnam, and to keep his sanity during the ordeal, he played four hours of mental golf daily on the giant movie screen in his mind, working his way through the course in vivid, step-by-step detail, never missing a shot. When the war was over and he was finally able to return to the game, he found his mental practice had paid off: the first time he stepped on a course after being released he shot an astounding 74.

Radio Days

If you listen to the radio, you are already a frequent visitor to the theatre of the mind. Perhaps the best way to demonstrate what a remarkable theatre this is by thinking for a minute about your favorite radio personality.

When you first started listening, you probably constructed a detailed picture of what this person looked like, based upon the sound of his or her voice. But what happened when you saw a picture of this person? Chances are you were surprised. It's not that disc jockeys or radio commentators are stranger looking than other people, it's just that their wonderful voices can conjure up a mental image that may not match their appearances.

In the years before television, millions of people sat glued to their radios each night listening to dramas, comedy hours, quiz shows. Ask people over 50 and they will tell you about the incredible worlds created by the masterful radio actors who could create a story so compelling that listeners were totally convinced it was real. The primary example of this is the Orson Welles radio version of the H.G. Wells story, "War of the Worlds." The formidable talents of Wells and his Mercury Theatre players convinced thousands of radio listeners that the Martians had landed—pandemonium was the result and there were several suicides. Welles later apologized publicly, saying he had no idea the effect the presentation would have.

Master the art of using your voice and you will find you can paint a richly detailed and positive picture of the benefits of your product or services. It works from a podium, in a conference room, or over the telephone. In fact, you might even come to prefer dealing with your clients over the telephone. One of the things I love about my work as a voice-over artist is that I can sell the most upscale products behind the microphone wearing an old shirt, jeans, and sneakers—I can also work from my home studio in my bathrobe if I want to. But best of all, when I am behind the microphone, I can be millions of women I could never play in person: older, younger, wacky, or straightlaced. I can get you to see me any way I want to—just by using the power of my voice.

Broadcasters Tip
Picture this

Radio is theatre of the mind. And so is the telephone. Through voice mastery and descriptive speech you can project images that are infinitely more vivid than anything captured by a camera. Weave colorful stores in great detail so your audience can "see" what you mean.

The Television Effect

If radio has taught us a lot about the power of the theatre of the mind, television has had an even more powerful impact on the way we communicate.

Roger Ailes, once media advisor to three U.S. Presidents, says that because of the influence of television, people expect even a casual social encounter to be as crisp and to-the-point as TV news. Because of this phenomenon, Ailes says long-winded people will soon be as extinct as the dinosaur. Like it or not, USA TODAY is the role model most often used by corporations when designing publications: colorful, brief, punchy.

Even radio is becoming more like television. When I did the news for CBS-Radio in New York we had to compress the news, sports, and weather into a 90-second broadcast. To keep the interest of your audience, you, too, must train yourself to edit your content down to the bare essentials, using colorful language and an animated style.

Painting Word Pictures

I have found that the easiest way to get your message across is first to do a dress rehearsal in the theatre of the mind for your most important audience—you. If you don't see it, they won't see it. You have to paint a vivid picture in your own mind before you can expect anyone else to see it.

For instance, if you are a sales person in the widget business, don't drone on about its technical specifications or how many awards it has won or what it looks like. Instead, talk about all the wonderful things this particular brand of widget has done—success stories (short ones), pithy quotes from satisfied customers, a word picture of this widget as one of the great ideas of western man.

A good realtor is a master of the theater of the mind. A three-bedroom, two-bath house with a fireplace is not just a piece of real estate, but a home where you can relax with friends and family. The yard you will mow into eternity becomes a greensward where you can watch your children frolic. The extra bedroom your mother-in-law will occupy becomes an office where you can write that best-seller you've always planned to write. Another master of the theater of the mind is a good lawyer. Gerry Spence, one of the most successful defense lawyers in the United States, has never lost a criminal case. He says his credibility with juries is not the result of acting or artifice, or of logic or intellect. The energy that convinces, he says, comes directly from the soul.

Listen to the great communicators. Before you can persuade anyone of anything, you must see it first in your own mind. You must believe in it.

Remember Robert Morse singing "I Believe In You" to his own image in the mirror in "How to Succeed in Business Without Really Trying"? He was on to something. Although the scene was a funny one, actors know the power of belief. Actress Julie Harris is quoted as saying: "The keynote of my acting is the ability to get caught up in a story, to really believe in a situation." Actor Morgan Freeman agrees. "Audiences believe what you believe," he says. "But it's all a matter of believing in yourself. If I believe in me, then you've got no choice. None at all."

Broadcasters Tip
Big production

The theatre of the mind likes a BIG production. When describing your product or service don't be shy. Be generous with descriptive adjectives. Show enthusiasm in your tone of voice.

Feelings

Some people confuse effective communication with being articulate. But it's not the words that convey the message, it's the feeling behind the words. A well educated speaker might attempt to hide his meaning and his feelings behind a wall of long, pretentious words. Ultimately, however, he will betray himself by his body language and tone of voice. A speaker with limited education can be very effective, just by telling us, simply, who he is and what he wants.

Revealing your feelings is the best way to establish credibility. This is because people get uncomfortable when they sense you want something from them, but don't know what it is. When you let people know your true intentions, however, you are much more likely to get the result you want. People—your audience, your client, your sales prospects—need to know why you are talking to them. This "why" is much more important than how we say it. In acting, this is called motivation. Since you now understand that every time you speak you are an actor in the theater of the mind, you will find that defining what it is you want to accomplish will be very helpful.

Broadcaster's Tip
Reveal your weakness

 The most loved broadcasters are those who seem relaxed and natural on the air. When delivering your presentations, don't aim for slick perfection. Audiences love it when you show your humanity and treat them warmly, as a friend.

Most corporations have "mission statements" to guide them— why shouldn't you? A mission statement is the clearly defined purpose behind what you say and it spells out what response you want. Your mission statement should be able to be reduced to one clear, concise sentence. And this applies whether you are speaking to one person over the telephone or 1,000 in an auditorium. Jed Harris, a famous Broadway producer of the 1930's and '40's, said that if you couldn't write why you wanted to see him on the inside of a match-book cover, he didn't want to see you. Harris was ahead of his time.

Lilly Walters, author of *Secrets of Successful Speakers*, says this "mission statement" is so important that if you can't state it in at least a few sentences, you should cancel the presentation (or the phone call) until you can figure it out.

How do you create this "mission statement"? Think of the word **CLEAR,** and then turn it into an acronym.

C stands for concise. Be specific about what it is you want to accomplish with this presentation or sales pitch or phone call.

L stands for limit. Limit the number of points you want to make to achieve your objective. It's better to cover a few points in depth than to bombard your audience with too much information.

E stands for easy-to-remember. You want the audience to remember in December what you said in June.

A stands for action. Tell your audience what you want them to do as a result of hearing you speak or talking to you—buy a certain product, vote a certain way, believe in a certain plan of action.

R stands for relevant. Never speak in generalities— make your presentation relevant to the needs and concerns of the audience.

Once you have what you think is a good mission statement, call a few friends who are unfamiliar with your topic and read it to them, asking them to listen carefully. Then change the subject. After a few minutes of general conversation, ask them what they remember of your mission statement. Don't correct them if they get the facts wrong— write down what they say and compare it with your original. According to Lilly Walters, only five percent of the people asked to participate in this experiment can remember the mission statement 10 minutes after hearing it. If your friends aren't getting your message, imagine how the audience will react.

Remember this: All audiences—of one or 1,000—are preoccupied. They are thinking about their own problems, or what they are going to have for dinner, or how they can meet next month's bills. It's your job to break through this wall of preoccupation and get them to listen to you.

You Must Remember This . . .

√   That in the theater of the mind, you can create an experience for your audience, or listener, that will paint a vivid picture of what you are trying to accomplish.

√   That your ticket to the theater of the mind is the power of believing. Before you can convince anyone of anything, you have to convince yourself.

√   That television has influenced everyone's perceptions—and it is up to you to be colorful, brief, and believable—just like your favorite news anchor or commentator.

√   That your credibility depends on how well you can reveal the truth about yourself and why you are speaking. And that truth has to be concise. It has to be CLEAR.

6

Play Your Voice Like A Finely Tuned Instrument

As Mark Twain was getting dressed one morning, he discovered that buttons were missing from all his shirts. He flew into a rage, cursing like a sailor, only to discover his very proper Victorian wife standing in the doorway glaring at him. To express her disapproval, she slowly and carefully repeated every obscene and profane word without a trace of emotion. When she was through, she stood silently, hoping to have thoroughly shamed her husband. But it was to no avail. Twain just smiled wryly, puffed on his cigar, and said, "My dear, you have the words but you just don't have the music."

In this chapter, you will learn how to add more music to your words through vocal pitch, tone, and inflection, the elements that help you put emotion and feeling into the way you speak. The voice is a modular instrument, comprised of a number of different qualities that can be mixed and matched to create an infinite variety of character and moods.

The Vocal Elements Are:

Pitch   from high to low

Inflection   the amount of fluctuation

	between your highest and lowest pitch
Tone	an emotion registered in the voice such as warm and friendly, cold and detached, businesslike and authoritative
Tempo	speed of speech
Rhythm	syncopated, lilting, staccato, or legato (notice the musical terminology)
Placement	where the voice comes from, such as the nose, the head, the throat

(In some cases a regional or foreign accent is also considered a vocal element. If you have either one, you might want to consider working with a speech coach to eliminate it, since any kind of accent often causes preconceptions in the mind of the listener.)

To create a different sound, all you need to do is make some adjustments to one or two of these vocal elements at a time.

For example, record yourself reading the sentence "**I am going for a walk**."

For the first reading, make your voice high-pitched. Then try it with a lower pitch. Now use no inflection whatsoever—make your voice totally flat. Now speak as though it were a question, not a statement. And, finally, put a downward inflection at the end. Can you hear how each of these elements affects that simple sentence?

Let's look at each of these elements.

• **Pitch** is very important. Consider how you feel about someone with a high-pitched voice—does he sound credible? Does a woman with a low-pitched voice sound overtly sexy or just professional?

• **Inflection** depends on pitch. If you eliminate all pitch variation, your voice sounds flat and monotonous. A study has shown that salesmen with more inflection in their voices sell more.

• **Tone**, and being aware of it, is vital in the voice-improvement process. Everyone has a basic tone in his natural speaking voice that conveys a certain emotion. I hope your underlying vocal tone is happy and pleasant. If you sound depressed and tired or angry and annoyed, it is going to come through.

• **Tempo** is equally important. Sales studies show that faster talkers are perceived as more intelligent, objective, knowledgeable, credible and persuasive. What about slow talkers? In today's fast-paced world, slow talkers can be annoying. Of course, in the United States, there are regional differences in the rate of speech. People in the South tend to speak more slowly than those in the North, but no matter where you are from, you can do a lot to increase your rapport with friends and business associates by matching their rate of speech. This simple maneuver will put the slow talker at ease and keep the fast talker from becoming irritable.

• Speech **rhythm** is another variable. Staccato speakers sound like James Cagney delivering his famous "You dirty rat..." line—everything comes in short, punchy bursts. The legato style is smooth and flowing, sounding more polished, poised, and in-control.

• What is **placement**? A well-placed voice resonates from the "facial mask." Examples of bad placement are throwing the voice into the nose (nasal-sounding speech) or too far down in the throat.

Let's analyze these vocal elements so that you can get more flexibility into your voice.

Pitch

Before you can begin shaping your voice to be more persuasive and create a variety of moods and emotions, you must determine whether or not you are speaking within your natural pitch. Voices come in a variety of natural pitches—some higher, some lower. One is no better or worse than another, yet often people are unnecessarily harsh on themselves because they feel their natural voice is pitched too high or too low. You wouldn't say a flute was any better or worse than a saxophone, would you? Like instruments, all voices can be beautiful if they are properly played.

In order for you to appreciate your natural pitch, you must first learn where it is. Dr. Morton Cooper, a Hollywood voice coach, has developed some simple exercises to help you do this. According to Dr. Cooper, the best way to find your natural pitch is to hum a few bars of a simple song like "Happy Birthday." The pitch at which you naturally hum is the same pitch at which you should speak.

When you hum, you should feel a slight buzz around your nose and lips. This is the area known as the "facial mask." When you are speaking from the mask in your natural voice, your voice is at its most focused and powerful. You will sound as though you have more energy—and you won't have to force or push your voice to be understood.

To get an idea of what it feels like to speak from the facial mask, Dr. Cooper suggests alternating between speaking and humming. When you have mastered this, see if you can SAY the words to the song, keeping the same voice level.

Did you try it? How did it feel? Did you notice a difference between your humming voice and the way you usually speak? This exercise can tell you if you are speaking above or below your natural pitch.

Speaking outside your natural pitch can strain your voice. Practice humming throughout the day to remind yourself to speak within your natural pitch. Another way to check yourself is to hum and then say your name. Since you are so used to saying your name, you will probably say it in your habitual pitch. Hum a little to find your optimal pitch, then try it again, keeping the hum and your name within the same pitch and tone.

Saying certain words can also improve vocal resonance, soften nasality, and bring your voice to its natural pitch. Dr. Cooper's two favorites are the words "right" and "no." He suggests raising your hands over your head and saying these two words with energy until you feel the buzz. Once you have mastered "talking on the buzz" you can be sure your voice is primed and ready whenever you have to sound "on."

After you do these exercises, you may feel as though you are speaking too loudly. You are not—it just sounds that way to you because you are now speaking in the facial mask. Tape record your voice before and after doing these exercises. You should hear a notice-able improvement.

Inflection

If you discovered in your vocal evaluation that you did not sound definite enough, if it was difficult to tell when a thought was completed, you did not sound believable, or you sounded as if you were asking for audience approval, pay special attention to this section.

If you feel that people don't take you as seriously as you would like, it may be because you end your sentences as though you are asking a question. Upward inflections can be a habit you adopted early in your career when you may have felt insecure about making a firm statement.

At the downward end of the inflection spectrum are those who keep the voice as flat as possible and end all sentences on a downward note. This habit is often adopted by those who feel that to get ahead, you have to keep your emotions under control. They try to force their voices lower to project a more authoritative image. The result is not what they think—it is a lifeless, monotonous voice. Left undetected, these vocal habits can make your voice annoying or boring—or both. If you discovered in your voice evaluation that your voice goes up or down when it shouldn't, the very fact that you are now aware of the problem should begin to cure it. The two exercises that follow will help you to achieve a more flexible and musical voice.

1   Hum a few bars of "Happy Birthday" to find the buzz, just as you did in the exercises earlier in this chapter. Now count from one to 10. Now go up a few tones and count from one to 10 again. Go up even higher. Now go as high as you can—if your voice feels painful or strained, do not go any higher. When you reach as high as you can comfortably go, count to 10 again.

2   Hum again to find your optimal pitch. When you find it, say "I am going for a walk." Keep repeating the sentence, pitching it successively lower until you reach your lowest comfortable pitch. Now hum yourself back to your optimal pitch and repeat the sentence in successively higher tones until you hit the top of your range.

Tone

Your tone of voice mirrors your emotional state and physical well-being. If your emotional state is positive, and you are feeling strong and healthy, your tone of voice will be upbeat, energetic, and enthusiastic. But when you are down, your negative emotions can tend to leak through and people can hear it in your voice. You want to make the right impression at all times, however, no matter what may be going on in your personal life or behind the scenes at work. The tips that follow will help you do this.

1   **Smile**
A smile on your face puts a smile in your voice. It works even when you're in a terrible mood. Keep a mirror by your phone to make sure there's a smile on your face before you pick up the receiver.

2   **Keep a beautiful picture of a child by the phone**
Any child will do. If it's your own child, so much the better. Ask yourself how long this child would stay upset about the thing that is troubling you. Tune into their joy, their spontaneity, their happiness.

3   **Say a key word**
A key word is any word that helps you access a desired emotional state. "Love" is a powerful key word. Say it over and over out loud, focusing deeply on its meaning and hear how your voice becomes softer and warmer as you speak.

4   **Change your body language**
Much research has been done by practitioners of the science of NLP (Neurolinguistic programming) about how physiology effects mental state. Actors use gestures and mannerisms to help them change their tone of voice. Note the

body language of anger: a clenched fist. Slamming your hand on the table. Throwing something. Stomping around. Now note the body language of love. A warm smile. An outstretched hand. A gentle touch. Try changing your physiology the next time you're feeling down. You'll be amazed at the results.

5   **Imagine you are enjoying a candlelight dinner with the person on the other end of the phone**
"Would you like a glass of Pinot Noir with that box of widgets, sir?" If this image makes you laugh, great! You're on the right track.

6   **Take a short, brisk walk outside**
You'll breathe more deeply, releasing pent up tension. The mere act of changing your scenery will help you change your state of mind.

7   **Keep fresh flowers by your desk**
Dr. Andrew Weil, bestselling author of several books on health and healing, says keeping fresh flowers where you can see and appreciate them can lift your spirits and have a therapeutic effect on health, and consequently on the sound of your voice.

8   **Tape record your voice**
To improve the way you sound you must hear yourself as others hear you. The only way to do this is to listen to your voice on tape. The voice you hear inside your head is not your true voice. It's distorted by the bones of your skill. By listening to yourself on tape, you'll get an

accurate impression of the way you sound to others. Do you sound angry or tired? Is this the voice you want your customers to hear? The awareness may make you cringe, but it can motivate you to make some positive and productive changes that will have a powerful impact on the way you come across to others.

Here are some exercises to help you practice changing your tone of voice at will. As we learned in an earlier chapter, you can do this easily by giving yourself an auditory cue (key word), a visual cue (mental image), and a kinesthetic cue (body language)

Warm and Friendly

The first tone we will work on is **Warm and Friendly**.

The **Key Word** is "**Tender**." Say this word three times slowly, with as much feeling as you can muster.

Now focus on a **Mental Image:** What image does the word "tender" call to mind? A lover's caress? A mother and her child? A mouth-watering filet mignon? It's up to you.

The **Body Language** for "warm and friendly" is **Relaxed.** To achieve this, take a few deep breaths and let the tension drain from your body. To sound warm and friendly, you also need to **Smile**. Not one of those celebrity all-teeth smiles, but a relaxed, gentle smile. Until you get into the habit of smiling while speaking, keep a mirror handy so you can observe yourself while on the phone. Always smile *before* you pick up the receiver and greet your caller.

Authoritative

The next tone to try is **Authoritative**.

The **Key Word** is "**Respect**." Say this word three times slowly until you capture a **Mental Image**.

The **Body Language** for an authoritative tone is posture so good it's positively military—think of an officer standing at attention. Your eyes count in this one, too. They should be intense and focused.

You Must Remember This . . .

√ That your voice is a modular instrument composed of pitch, inflection, tone, tempo, rhythm, and placement. Changing one or any combination of these elements gives you vocal variety.

√ That humming a few bars of a simple song is the best way to find your optimal pitch. When you feel a buzz around your mouth and nose, you know you've got it.

√ That you can make your voice more expressive and cure a monotone by speaking above and below your natural pitch to find your highest and lowest comfort zone.

√ That your voice will convey any emotion by identifying a key word you associate with the emotion and reinforcing it with strong mental imagery and the appropriate body language.

7

Tempo! Rhythm! Placement!

In this chapter, we will be covering more vocal elements: tempo (or rate of speech), rhythm, and vocal placement.

Tempo (aka Rate of Speech)

Let's begin with speaking rate. How fast or slow you talk is more important than you might think. In a study published in the *Journal of Personal Selling and Sales Management*, psychologists Robert Peterson, Michael Cannito, and Steven Brown analyzed how rate of speech and voice characteristics affect selling ability. They studied 21 salesmen, who made presentations for a household product to 26 housewives.

Their findings were surprising. The faster a salesperson spoke (within a "normal" range), the more he sold. The average rate of speech is about 150 words per minute, but for the successful salesman it was about 247 words per minute.

As an added benefit, the faster-talking salesmen were also perceived as more intelligent, objective, knowledgeable, credible, and persuasive. Interestingly, the salesmen achieved this increased rate of speed not by speaking the actual words faster, but by compressing the pauses between the words and sentences and by using contractions. For example, the phrase, "Do you have a place where we can sit down?" became "Dyave a place where wecn siddown?"

Here's how you can find out if your speaking rate is slower or faster than normal. Go back to the tape you made of the scripted portion of your voice evaluation and time it. The scripted voice evaluation contains 158 words. A person speaking at an average rate will complete the script in about one minute. If you are in sales, and want to see what the optimum rate of 247 words per minute feels like, get a stop watch and try to read the script in 39 seconds. You may not be able to read that quickly, but try speaking a little faster and see if you close more sales.

Broadcaster's Tip
Compress space

When I do commercials, I often have to read very quickly. The timing of commercials is very precise: 20 seconds, 58 seconds, a minute 42 seconds. I have to be right on the money—not one second over—or I have to record the whole thing again. Whenever I need to increase my rate of speech, I don't focus on saying the words more quickly, I think of eliminating unnecessary pauses and compressing the space between the words—just like the salesmen in the study.

Look back at the script, on page 26, that you read for your

voice evaluation. Let's start with the first paragraph:

> **"Many people think that communicating effec-
> tively is merely a matter of finding and using the
> right magic words. They believe that using certain
> words in the right order will get them the results
> they want."**

The first step is to mark your script so that you pause at the right place only when necessary for breath and meaning.

Earlier, we learned that the proper place to breathe is at the end of a thought, even if it comes in the middle of a sentence. Go through the following paragraph now, marking the proper places to pause.

> **"Many people think that communicating effec-
> tively** *(pause)* **is merely a matter of finding and
> using the right magic words."**

If you have good breath control, try to read the entire sentence without a pause. If that is too much for you, pausing after "communicating effectively" creates a sense of anticipation regarding what you are about to say, and is a handy place to grab a little air.

Practice the sentence a few times, imagining that the space between the words is getting smaller and smaller. Now go on to the next sentence.

> **"They believe that using certain words in the right
> order,** *(pause)* **will get them the results they
> want."**

The only place you should pause to breathe here is after "order." Be sure you link the rest of the words together tightly.

Now on to the next sentence.

"Unfortunately, these people are living in a dream world."

Although in the written script there is a comma after "unfortunately," it can be eliminated from the spoken version. If you are reasonably healthy, you should easily be able to say the entire sentence in one breath.

The next sentence is

"Scientific research tells us that attempting to persuade by words alone is about as effective as trying to chop down a tree with a Swiss Army knife."

The best place to pause for breath is after "words alone." See if you can make the rest of the sentence flow together.

Remember, relaxed, natural breathing is a key factor in helping us read more quickly and smoothly. If you exhale too much air before you speak, you will be forced to pause repeatedly to catch your breath. Choppiness can also be caused by emotional stress, which leads to muscle tension and a restriction of natural breathing. If this happens to you, review the breathing exercises in Chapter 2.

While speaking faster can make you seem more intelligent and persuasive, there are times when fear or nervousness can turn a person into a motor-mouth, causing him or her to race through a presentation completely out of control.

This happens when the stress of public speaking causes an inexperienced speaker to panic. As a result, the heart beats faster and the speaker goes into a state of overdrive that he or she cannot control.

As the adrenaline surges through the speaker's body, he tends to leap to his feet and plunge headlong into his speech.

To control a stress-induced motor-mouth, try some of the stress reducing breathing exercises you learned in Chapter 1. When practiced regularly they will help you remain calm and relaxed while waiting in the wings before your speech.

I Got Rhythm (But Have You?)

The next vocal characteristic is rhythm. Rhythm ranges from short, staccato-like bursts to a smooth, flowing delivery known as legato.

Actor James Cagney was famous for his staccato delivery, and more recently, presidential candidate Steven Forbes exemplified this rhythm. Using a staccato rhythm can be effective if you want to emphasize a point. Johnny Cochran did this during the O.J. Simpson trial when he said, in a rap-like rhythm, "If it doesn't fit, you must acquit." Famous legato speakers include Bing Crosby, Ricardo Montalban, Eartha Kitt, and Elizabeth Taylor. You will know if speech rhythm is a problem for you if you discovered in your voice evaluation that people tune you out. Perhaps your evaluators said you sounded singsongy or boring.

An enjoyable way to develop a more varied speaking rhythm is through an exercise called "remote control." To do it, sit down in front of a television set with a hand-held remote control channel changer.

Flip quickly through the channels, spending about 15 seconds on each station. As you go, try to imitate every sound you hear. It doesn't matter if it is a man or a woman or a child, a cartoon, an animal, music, or a sound effect. If you hit a foreign language station and they are speaking another language, fake it. The exact words are not important—you are trying to capture the rhythm and texture of the speech and reach for sounds you would not normally make.

Don't spend too long on any one channel. Keep flipping through and stretching your voice up and down, inside and out. Don't push yourself to the point of pain—if your throat starts to hurt, switch channels and try another sound. This exercise is enormously entertaining and some of the sounds you make are sure to surprise you. For added fun, ask any children in the house to join in.

Broadcasters Tip
Tape and ape

Record your favorite TV and radio personalities and imitate them. By trying to replicate their sound, you'll learn a lot about pacing, tonality and body language.

Placement Pointers

The next VoiceShaping® component is placement, which can also be thought of as "vocal focus."

In the exercises that follow, you will learn how to achieve a fuller, richer, more resonant voice. You will learn how to amplify and project your voice without straining . And you will learn some other tricks that can help you have a deeper, more mature and authoritative sound, or a younger, lighter, more innocent sound.

When you speak, a column of air from the lungs vibrates the

larynx, causing sound. This sound then travels to the mouth, where it is formed into words by the lips, teeth, and tongue. For people with thin, weak voices, the process stops here. They tend to use the mouth as a resonating chamber, and by doing so, lose half their vocal effectiveness.

To get the kind of rich, vibrant sound you want, you have to learn to place your voice in the triangular area that stretches between your two sinuses and your mouth. This is the area known as the facial mask. Within the sinus cavities are hollow bones that reverberate and enlarge the sound of your voice. The sinuses are your body's natural amplifiers, your own personal public address system.

In his book, *The How-To of Great Speaking*, Hal Persons describes a vocal placement technique that will help you get a richer, more resonant voice in practically no time at all.

Imagine that you have a hole in the top of your head about one inch in diameter. Projecting from this hole is a tube about 10 inches long. As you speak, visualize sending your voice up past your mouth, nose, and eyes and out through the tube. See each word coming up through the tube and bouncing off the ceiling.

To test this technique, tape record yourself speaking normally and then projecting through the top of your head. See if you can notice the difference.

As you do this exercise, do not push or strain in any way. If resonance and projection are a problem for you, practice speaking through the top of your head for a few minutes every day. A good way to do this is to tape record yourself reading aloud from a newspaper or trade journal. If you can practice with an actual sales script or other presentation, so much the better. Hearing the rich, resonant difference in your voice will keep you motivated. After a few weeks, speaking from the top of your head will become second nature.

I learned the power of vocal focus when I interviewed actors who do the voices for cartoons. These talented people can make themselves sound like a pig, a car, a superhero, or anything else at the drop of a hat. These actors confirmed that changing the sound of the voice is often merely a matter of visualizing that the voice is coming from a different part of the body. For example, to raise your pitch and sound younger, imagine you are speaking from somewhere in the vicinity of your eyes. Tape record yourself at your customary pitch and then speaking from your eyes. Practice shifting back and forth until you hear a distinct difference. Shifting the vocal focus up to the eyes is useful for anyone who feels his or her voice is too heavy or deep or who wants to sound younger. This imagery is especially valuable for speakers who have been suffering from vocal strain trying to push their voices below their optimal pitch in an attempt to sound more authoritative and commanding.

To sound more authoritative and commanding, lower your mental focus. Imagine that you are speaking from below your neck, somewhere around your solar plexus. You can make this easier by placing one hand on your chest as you speak. Men should place their hands on the solar plexus, beneath the ribs, and women should place their hands above the rib cage, on the sternum.

Now say, "If I could talk from my chest I would sound like this." Focus on the area beneath your hand. Feel the vibrations as you speak. Tape record this exercise, going back and forth between your normal speaking voice and your "chest voice."

Let's try another exercise. Shift all your attention to your nose. To make this easier, pinch your nostrils and say "If I could talk from my nose I would sound like this." Focus hard on your nose and try to sound as nasal as possible. You should feel your nose vibrating beneath your fingers. There is no practical reason why you would want to sound as silly as this, except to amuse children, but this exercise will give you the idea of sounds that are possible merely by shifting your vocal focus.

Speaking of nasality, studies have shown that a whiney, nasal voice is one of the most annoying vocal problems. In fact, the lush-voiced Grace Kelly started her acting training with a voice evaluation that described her voice as "improperly placed," and "very nasal." After extensive work with a vocal coach, her voice became so mellow that it was described by a Hollywood journalist as "cream of tomato soup."

In her book *Talk to Win*, Dr. Lillian Glass suggests testing yourself for nasality by pinching the bridge of your nose between your thumb and index finger and saying "ba, ba, ba." If you feel a vibration or buzzing, you have a problem with nasality.

Here are a couple of things you can do. Dr. Glass says most people sound nasal because they do not open their jaws enough when they speak. They tend to clench down on their jaws, aggravating the problem. To make sure your jaws are in the proper position, pretend you have a dime propped lengthwise between your back teeth. Your back teeth should not touch. Don't try this with a real dime—you could swallow it. Pinch the bridge of your nose again and repeat "ba, ba, ba," imagining that the dime is still keeping those back teeth apart. Feel the difference?

There is such a thing as being not nasal enough. It is a condition known as "de-nasal" and makes a person sound stuffed up, as with a head cold. If people often ask if you are suffering from a cold even when you are not, you could be suffering from a nasal obstruction or enlarged adenoids. You should see an ear, nose, and throat specialist to get help for this type of condition.

Broadcaster's Tip
Vocal strain

If you feel you are suffering from vocal strain, get your throat checked by a doctor—preferably a board certified ear, nose and throat specialist. Doing so will rule out any medical problems and put your mind at ease. Signs of vocal strain include: persistent hoarseness or raspiness; frequent sore throats; a weak voice which tires easily; a dry, scratchy-sounding voice; and a voice which sounds strained. When doing vocal exercises never do anything that hurts. If you feel strain while doing any of the exercises in this book, stop immediately!

You Must Remember This . . .

√   That the average rate of speech is about 150 words per minute—increasing your rate to 247 words per minute can make you a better sales person.

√   That to increase your rate of speech, you must eliminate unnecessary pauses and compress the space between your words.

√   That an unnatural speaking rhythm can make people lose interest in what you have to say. Practice by talking back to your television!

√   That placing your voice in the facial mask can help you project without strain and give you a rich, fuller, more resonant voice.

√   That to reduce nasality, keep your jaws relaxed and unclenched as you speak. Imagine that you are speaking with a dime wedged between your back teeth.

8

How To Be A Stress-Free Speaker

Did you know that the fear of public speaking is the number one fear? Worse even than the fear of death? Yet just about everyone has experienced some degree of speech fright at some time in their life, even those whose speaking skills we admire. Actors, athletes and public figures know all about the delicate balance between anxiety and energy. Sir Laurence Olivier, Helen Hayes, Luciano Pavarotti, Carly Simon, Barbra Streisand and Willard Scott all admitted they suffered from nervousness and stage fright. Speech fright can strike in front of an audience of any size, even over the phone.

In this chapter, I will explore the cause of speech fright and the most effective methods I have found to deal with the problem. I would like to alert you in advance that you might find the tone of this chapter to be a bit different than that in the rest of the book. That's because I will be introducing some psychological principles that may seem out of place in what is otherwise a how-to manual. But I include them because understanding and working with these principles has been vital to both my professional and personal development.

What Causes Speech Fright?

To begin with, it is important to understand that the symptoms of speech fright—the pounding heart, sweaty palms, trembling voice and anxious feelings—are a perfectly normal reaction to acute stress. These unpleasant, scary and even debilitating symptoms are actually the symptoms of a stress-induced adrenaline rush. There are several proven techniques that can be used to burn off the excess adrenaline before a presentation and make public speaking a more comfortable experience, and I'll share these methods a little later on in this chapter.

A few exercises may be all you need if your speech fright is mild. But if your fear of public speaking is affecting your work, if you avoid speaking in public, if you lose sleep before a presentation or must resort to tranquilizers or other extreme measures, then it is vital to understand the psychological root of the problem.

The Psychology Of Speech Fright

Speaking before an audience is one of the most consciousness-raising experiences a person can have. Step into the limelight and you are flooded with awareness. Whenever we speak in public, we risk reputation and career advancement. We are afraid of appearing unprofessional or foolish, of saying the wrong thing, of embarrassing ourselves or making a mistake.

We worry about the audience. Will they be receptive, tune us out, or throw rotten fruit? We worry about the medium. Will the microphone work? Will the multimedia presentation crash and burn? Will we look okay on television? Some people feel ashamed and inadequate. Others fear failure, criticism and humiliation. As these feelings mount, the speaker feels as if he must flee the platform or die.

Enlightening and entertaining others, helping them by sharing information that has been carefully researched and developed should be a positive, uplifting experience. Yet why does something so good fill so many people with dread?

I found many of the answers to my questions in the work of Brazilian psychoanalysts, Dr. Norberto Keppe, founder of the International Society of Analytical Trilogy (Integral Psychoanalysis) and his associate Dr. Claudia Pacheco. I met Drs. Keppe and Pacheco several years ago when they were living and working in the United States and have been a student of Dr. Keppe's work ever since. Both have been instrumental in helping me understand the psychology of communication problems, and I am deeply grateful for their profound insight and support.

It is difficult to do justice to Dr. Keppe's work in a few brief pages. He has developed his methodology during more than 30 years of clinical research and has published more than 25 books on the subject. Yet I will do the best I can, because I believe his insights provide the explanation to the cause and cure of speech fright

When Dr. Keppe investigated the inner core of the human personality, he found that human nature was profoundly different than what Freud believed. Keppe observed that our essential nature, or Being, is oriented toward life, love, truth and beauty; not toward death and destruction as Freud proposed. He concluded that we become stressed and sick because we are not true to our inner self. We adopt destructive attitudes that go against our essential nature, which is good, beautiful and truthful. Fortunately, though, we are blessed with consciousness, an inner sense of awareness that enables us to perceive these destructive attitudes so we can correct them and get ourselves back on track.

Keppe found that we distort reality by attempting to deny our fallibility. We prefer to fantasize that it is possible to be godlike, perfect and error free. Thus, we set all kinds of unreasonable expectations for our performance and are devastated when we are unable to meet them. Many phobic speakers suffer from this exaggerated form of perfectionism, which Keppe calls *theomania*- the hidden desire in all human hearts to be other than we are. According to Keppe, phobic individuals are not so much afraid of speaking as they are afraid of accepting the consciousness of their fallibility which public speaking might reveal.

Another of the core concepts discovered by Dr. Keppe, which relates to speech fright, is the phenomenon of inversion. Keppe noted that his patients who engaged in addictive, alienating or dangerous acts did so because they mistakenly believed these acts were beneficial in some way. Conversely, he noted that people have a tendency to resist, and even attempt to destroy, what is clearly best for them in life. "Love hurts" is an example of this.

Inversion, then, leads us to resist those things which may be challenging, but which ultimately are good for our personal and professional growth. Public speaking clearly fits this category. A good presentation is an act of love and dedication. It can take days or even weeks to prepare even the shortest talk, and all the while the speaker must struggle with procrastination. Then he must find a way to present the material in a manner that is meaningful to the audience, using every trick at his disposal to capture and engage their attention. He must set his own ego aside and speak to the audience in a way they can understand. And despite his nervousness and fear, he must deliver his talk without putting them to sleep. Despite the hard work, the benefits of giving a successful presentation are great. But if we feel that contributing to others is somehow injurious or bad, we will never allow ourselves to put forth the effort required to reap the rewards.

Conquering The Physical Symptoms of Speech-Fright

The physical symptoms we associate with speech fright, scary as they may be, are actually symptoms of a temporary overabundance of stress-related hormones in the blood stream. These hormones— adrenaline and noradrenaline—affect our entire body. When they flood the bloodstream in response to stress, our breathing becomes shallow and more rapid, our heartbeat increases, pupils dilate and muscles become tense. For more information about the relationship between hormones, stress and physical illness read *Healing Through Consciousness: Theomania, The Cause Of Stress"* by Dr. Claudia B. Pacheco. Information on where to find this important book can be found in Appendix B.

Mike is a subscriber to my free VoiceCoach newsletter (*www.greatvoice.com*). He wrote to me after landing a "dream job" as a TV sports commentator. Unfortunately, he found that while he was on camera his throat would tense up and he would feel, as he put it, "a desperate need to swallow." Sometimes this sensation would cause him to stumble and lose his place while on the air.

Mike's "desperate need to swallow," is a stress related symptom. As Dr. Pacheco writes in *Healing Through Consciousness*, when we feel fear or anger, our body secretes excess adrenaline, noradrenaline and acetylcholine. This directly affects the secretion of saliva, (either too much or too little) affecting in turn the hydration of the mucus membranes of the mouth and throat, causing dryness and the uncomfortable symptoms Mike described.

I asked Mike what his new job meant to him. He said "Recognition, power, success and excitement, a chance to do what I always wanted." He also associated the job with an important opportunity for professional advancement and personal development, a milestone in his career, the attainment of a long-cherished goal.

The fact that his "desperate need to swallow" made him fear his speech would be interrupted can be interpreted as Mike's unconscious attempt to "interrupt" his professional development and impede himself from reaching his goals.

Note Mike's inversion. Rationally he knew the promotion was a good thing, that it would mean career advancement, recognition and success. But emotionally he rejected the advancement, reacting with fear and stress. Being on TV put Mike in touch with two opposing attitudes: one that wanted to move ahead in his career and one that wanted to be held back.

Why Do So Many People Fear Success?

Have you ever wondered why so many people seem to fear success? Consider this. When we decide to move ahead in life, to accomplish something truly worthwhile, we inevitably must face challenges and solve problems. There are new skills to master. Take our friend Mike, for example. In his old job on the radio he was an expert sportscaster. But for his new job on TV, he needed to develop a whole new set of skills and face new challenges.

The more positive and worthy the endeavor, the more likely we are to come face to face with the stuff we are made of. The more we try to grow, the more we are forced to confront our flaws, the gaps in our knowledge, our self-importance, our petty jealousies, our relationship problems, and even those problems outside of our control in society and the world around us. These moments of truth can be a painful reality check, especially if we have harbored fantasies or grandiose ideas about ourselves. But clearly, the more we are willing to look at how far *off* track we are, the more we will be able to keep ourselves on course.

Why Am I So Afraid Of The Audience?

Many speakers say they feel nervous because they are fearful of the audience. They fear being judged, criticized, or forced to confront a barrage of hostile questions. But while some audience members may be critical and even hostile, most people who come to hear us speak are well intentioned. They want to learn something. They want us to succeed. Otherwise why would they spend valuable time and even money to hear us speak? If you are well prepared, if you know your stuff and know your audience and if you design your presentation to meet their needs, then rationally, you should be well received.

But if you still feel the audience is against you, you may be experiencing a common psychological phenomenon known as projection. Here, we unconsciously project attitudes that originate within ourselves onto others because we prefer not to see those attitudes within ourselves.

For example, if we associate an audience with hostility and criticism when there is no apparent reason for doing so and if we associate public speaking with professional growth and development, we are most likely projecting our self-critical attitudes outwardly onto others. It means that we prefer not to see how harshly we criticize ourselves and how, (because of our inversion) we are hostile to the growth and development that public speaking represents.

I have had the opportunity to observe many people in many countries while working with them on their voice and presentation skills. And I have had the opportunity to deeply analyze my own communication problems, fears and failures. One core truth emerges: **a critical audience is nothing compared to the ferocity with which we criticize and bash ourselves**. In speaking and in life, we set superhuman standards of perfection for ourselves and then attempt to censor any evidence that shows us we are not as we imagine ourselves to be.

I have trained entire roomfuls of people where every single person was convinced that their own voice was positively awful, even if their voice was pleasant and good. It took me years of getting paid for doing voice-overs before I could admit that my voice was probably okay, and even now, I sometimes have my doubts. Just about everyone thinks their voice is too nasal, though few voices actually are. I've heard women with deep, rich voices say they think their voice is squeaky and high. I've seen men who speak too slowly insist they talk too fast. I've heard strong, effective speakers tell me they thought they sounded wimpy and weak.

In order to grow in any field, you need to get objective feedback. That's why even world class athletes and performers have coaches. Balanced, supportive feedback— providing a realistic picture of how you are perceived by others— is vital for anyone who wants to attain voice mastery.

Managing Adrenaline: The Essentials

As we saw previously, adrenaline causes many of the uncomfortable symptoms of speech fright. It is the fight or flight hormone whose purpose is to help us react to danger. But unfortunately adrenaline can flood the bloodstream at the most inopportune times, causing your body to react as if it must run from a snarling tiger when all you have to do is give a talk to your ski club!

There are many things you can do to cope with the symptoms of speech fright. Techniques such as physical exercises and deep breathing are useful, but they are not nearly as effective as working with the emotional root of the problem.

Dr. Pacheco says that when a person or a situation makes us nervous it is because they remind us of something we do not want to see within ourselves. The minute we feel angry, frustrated or irritated she suggests we stop, think and free associate. Free association works like this. Let's say you have to make a big presentation to Ms. Tough, a new client. You've met her before and she makes you very nervous. To free associate, think about Ms. Tough and notice what comes to mind.

Maybe you think she's very critical, that she dislikes you or wants to see you fail.

Now turn the ideas you have about Ms. Tough around and try to put them inside you. When you do, you'll see that Ms. Tough is probably showing you some things about yourself that you would rather not see. This process is called *interiorization*. Ms. Tough may indeed be a very critical person. But her critical nature would not bother you much if you were willing to see the same critical attitude within yourself. Dr. Pacheco assures us that free association and interiorization will help calm us down, not just before a presentation but at any time.

Next, get back on track by realigning yourself with your highest and best intention. Before going in front of any audience take a moment to focus on what you have to give. Think about how your message will help those who hear you; note how it will enrich them or improve their lives. Get firm about your decision to give of yourself, to help and be of service in any way you can. Step forward with the conviction that even if you stumble or make a mistake, even if your delivery is less than perfect, if your intention is sincere, you *will* be a success. Positive, uplifting, loving thoughts such as these have the power to completely obliterate fear.

Managing Adrenaline: The Particulars

1   **Get moving**
    Burn the adrenaline off by getting some exercise. Take a brisk walk around the building or up and down the hall.

2   **Push a wall**
    Actors use this exercise to beat stage fright.

Stand a few feet away from the wall and carefully lunge against it, one leg forward, one leg back, making sure you do not strain your knees in any way. While in the lunge position, attempt to push the wall away from you with your hands. Push as hard as you can, then relax. Alternate pushing and relaxing until you feel your stress level diminish. By the way, if you succeed in actually pushing the wall over, give me a call. I know a director who's doing a re-make "Samson and Delilah" who wants to hear from you.

3   Do some secret isometrics

This is great when you can't get out of the room to exercise or push a wall. While waiting to speak, create muscle tension by sitting up in your chair and pressing your feet firmly into the ground. At the same time, press your arms against the sides of the chair or against your lap. Press the small of your back against the back of the chair. Hold this position for a long count of three. Then relax to a long count of three and repeat as needed. This exercise is great because it can be done in secret anywhere. Not only does it diminish nerves, it also helps increase physical vitality.

4   Make a joyful noise

Another great way to burn adrenaline is to speak or sing out loud. Practice your speech at full volume. Sing in the shower or in the car on the way to the event. Singing will also warm up your voice.

5   Cut back on caffeine before a presentation
Too much coffee or tea can rev you up and
make the symptoms of stress even worse.

6   Surround yourself with beauty
Some soothing music, a bouquet of flowers or a
few moments spent communing with nature will
help lift your spirits and inspire you.

7   Don't apologize for nervousness
Some speakers assume their nervousness must
be so obvious to others, they open their talk
with an apology. But nervousness feels worse
than it looks. The audience can't see your
pounding heart or sweaty palms so don't call it
to their attention. If you admit to being nervous,
the audience will become distracted from your
message and will worry whether you'll make it
through your talk.

8   If your voice trembles, breathe deeply
Muscle tension is constricting your diaphragm,
causing you to speak on insufficient air. Counter
this effect by breathing deeply before you begin
to speak. Doing so should give your voice all
the support it needs to come out clear and
strong.

9   Practice makes perfect
In her book "Secrets of Successful Speakers,"
Lilly Walters says that 75 percent of stage fright
can be reduced by rehearsal and preparation,
15 percent by deep breathing, and the remaining 10 percent by mental preparation. When
practicing, read the presentation through several

times to yourself. Then read it several times aloud, practicing in front of a mirror. Next, tape yourself while practicing on audio and video if possible. Finally, practice in front of friends and family members and ask for feedback.

10   Prepare to succeed
It is a good idea to gather at least seven times as much useful information as you will actually use. It was said that Winston Churchill took eight hours to write a 45-minute speech.

11   Visualize success
Supplement the run-through of your material with positive visualization. Athletes do this all the time and it has been proven to enhance performance. As soon as you are scheduled for a speaking engagement, set aside a few minutes daily to imagine yourself having a successful speaking experience. If you can, visit the site of your speech in advance. That way you can picture the room as it's going to look. If that's not possible, ask your host for a detailed description.

You Must Remember This . . .

√   That love conquers fear. Before giving a talk, align yourself with your highest and best intention. Think about how your message will help those who hear you. Step forward with the conviction that even if you stumble or make a mistake, even if your delivery is less than perfect, if you are well prepared and your intention is positive you *will* be a success.

√   That stress reduction techniques are useful in helping to control speech fright but they are not nearly as effective as working with the emotional root of the problem.

√   That the physical symptoms of speech fright are stress related and come from an exaggerated form of perfectionism and a wish to be error-free. People are not so much afraid of speaking as they are afraid of accepting the awareness of faults which public speaking might reveal.

√   That a critical audience is nothing compared to the ferocity with which we judge ourselves. It is very difficult to be objective about yourself. To improve your speaking skills, you must get balanced feedback from others

9

Hold Audience Attention

When you speak, do people listen? Or can you feel their attention wandering?

When you tell a joke, do people really laugh or do they just chuckle politely and look the other way, leaving you with the embarrassing feeling that you look foolish. When you tell a story, is it truly interesting or do people look restless, tap their fingers impatiently, and maybe even tell you to get to the point? Do you wish you were better at getting your ideas across? Do you sometimes suspect you are boring?

One of the best ways to capture and hold people's attention is through humor. The problem is, you can't make anyone laugh by trying to be funny. Just think of an amateur comic in a talent show; he comes on stage working at being funny, but the more desperate he is for laughs, the fewer he gets.

I doubt that you are intending to make a career of stand-up comedy. But I do believe anyone can learn to be funnier. The place to start is to rent a video of your favorite comic and watch it with a critical eye. Notice how easy it is to get involved in the act. You never doubt the comic's sincerity or feel he or she is trying to be funny. Note how the material is never emotionally neutral. Each bit within the act conveys a definite emotional attitude. Some of the most common themes are worry, anxiety, anger, confusion, or frustration. But whatever it is, the emotional attitude is always specific and focused. If the performer is any good, there should never be any doubt about the feeling being conveyed.

Communicating with humor is no different than any other form of communication. To be truly effective, you have to say it with feeling! Whether you are telling a joke or expressing your ideas in a sales letter or business presentation, you will find that people do not respond to words—they respond to the feelings and emotions behind your words. To get through to others, to really persuade and make them feel your point of view, you need to be perfectly clear about how you feel about what you are saying and about how you want them to feel as a result of listening.

Another thing to notice is that the funniest people are serious about being funny. It's not that they are necessarily deadpan, though sometimes they are. But whether they are ranting and raving or sharing their wry observations about the things they love and hate, they always come across to the audience as sincere. We believe them. They seem fully involved with their stories and jokes. And most importantly, they are passionate about communicating their point of view, however warped it may be.

Performers call this being committed to the material. Comic Richard Lewis, for example, is deadly serious about his anxiety. His entire act revolves around new ways to express his emotional angst. George Carlin is serious about his observations of the absurdities in the world around us. And Jay Leno is sincerely ticked off about stupidity. When he sees a stupid ad for a new microwave oven that can cook a meal in 10 seconds, he asks, "Are there really people who say, `Hey, I've been home for 10 seconds, where the hell is dinner?'"

By studying the comedy experts, we can also learn how to tell a better joke. You will notice that most stand-up acts are made up of a group of jokes strung together consisting of a series of set-ups and punch lines, all having to do with a particular subject about which the comic has very definite feelings and opinions.

The set-up is the straight part of the joke. It's not meant to be funny. Its purpose is to grab the audience and entice them to stay tuned for the punch line, or pay-off. The set-up is something the audience can relate to—an interesting question, a shocking statement, or anything that will pique their interest and draw them in. A good set-up should always be believable and short—no longer than two or three lines at most. The best comics never let you go for more than a few seconds without a laugh.

After the comic grabs the attention of the audience with the set-up, he hits them with the punch line. To be truly funny, a punch line should contrast sharply with the set-up. This contrast can come from a sudden or outrageous change of attitude, an exaggeration, an interesting twist or a change of direction.

Another form of humor is observations and comments on the world—but from a unique point of view. Jay Leno, for instance, noted that in 7-Eleven stores, there are $10,000 worth of security cameras guarding $2 worth of Twinkies. Jerry Seinfeld has noticed that women seem to need millions of cotton balls every day. They buy them by the truckload, he said, and two days later they need more.

If Your Jokes Aren't Going Over, Consider These Points . . .

1 Are you trying too hard? People get turned off when they feel someone wants something from them, even if it's only a laugh. The funniest people tell their stories spontaneously, as if they were

talking off the tops of their heads. They never make you feel you are being forced to listen. The bores tell their stories as if they are desperate for laughs.

2   Are you being clear? People will not laugh at something they do not understand. And they will not laugh if they are confused. You may be going over the head of your audience. Something that is hilariously funny to a group of computer programmers might bomb with a group of construction workers. Also consider the audience's mental state. If you are trying to entertain a group of drunken party animals, remember that their attention span and level of comprehension is greatly diminished.

3   Is your timing off? Don't interrupt a conversation just to tell a joke. This is not only rude, it's awkward, especially if the joke has nothing to do with what's being discussed. Humor should flow into the conversation naturally, otherwise you will risk looking like a show-off. Avoid, too, trying to tell jokes to someone who seems overwhelmed by business or personal matters. They probably won't appreciate your attempts at humor.

4   Are your jokes offensive? Unless you are 12 years old, avoid bathroom humor, racist or sexist jokes, jokes that are based on religious beliefs, disabilities, or country of origin.

5   Are you passionate about your story or joke, or are you on automatic pilot? Remember, an audience will spot a lack of enthusiasm in a matter of seconds and tune you out before you get to the punch line.

Here are some additional thoughts on laying an egg

It's not such a big deal. If you tell a joke and nobody laughs, you might feel embarrassed, but it won't kill you. Novice comics expect that as many as half of all their jokes will fall flat. They know that the perfection of their craft is an ongoing process that depends on trial and error in front of an audience.

Another important thing to remember when your attempts at humor fail is that it was the material that failed, not you. This distinction allows you to get back on your feet, dust yourself off, analyze what went wrong, and try again.

There are some things you can do, however, when you feel a joke or story is starting to crash and burn.

Here are some tips from comedy experts:

1   Keep going. The audience might be preoccupied—and it might take them a while to catch up with you. This is especially true at parties where people may be under the influence of alcohol.

2   Admit the obvious. Don't pretend you don't notice what's happening and try to cover up by smiling more and speeding up your story. Comics call this "calling" the situation and it can be very funny when they stop the show and admit the obvious. Late night talk show host David Letterman does this often, usually in the form of asides to Paul Schaefer.

3   Don't think of the experience in terms of failure. Think instead about how you will say it differently next time. The important thing is to keep practicing.

Try to tell at least one joke a day, preferably to a different person each day.

Broadcaster's Tip
Flop forward

To flop is an essential part of the creative process. Expect it. Welcome it. A flop gives you valuable feedback about audience response and helps you refine your presentation.

Once Upon A Time . . .

The ability to tell a compelling, memorable and spellbinding story is a talent we all admire. Everyone loves a good story and the ability to be a good storyteller can not only make you more popular in social circles, it can also greatly improve your business life.

Imagine being able to tell a story about your product or service and paint a clear, dynamic picture in the mind of a potential customer. Imagine feeling confident about your ability to express your ideas and concepts in a compelling and persuasive manner.

One of the best ways to improve your own storytelling ability is to study the techniques in one of the oldest forms of storytelling: the fairy-tale.

There are five steps in a good fairytale. Study these steps and see how you can apply them to a story of your own.

1 Set the stage—explain the situation simply. Use

vivid, colorful language to describe the players and the place.

2 Draw us immediately into a dilemma. Suggest a conflict your audience can relate to such as good guy vs. bad guy, a flawed character heading for a fall or the little guy fighting the noble fight against the powers-that-be. Clearly identify the good guys and the bad guys and make the hero appealing.

3 Set the audience up. Paint such a clear picture of the conflict that the listener will begin speculating from the very beginning about what the probable outcome will be. But always leave them guessing as to how the inevitable will happen.

4 Hold the listeners' attention by speaking their language. Build the story and draw the listener in by carefully and vividly describing each event as it unfolds. Create suspense by emphasizing a telling remark or a significant detail.

5 End the story with a clear moral, if there is one. Tie up the loose ends and leave each character accounted for.

Broadcaster's Tip
The essence of entertainment

"The essence of entertainment will not change. What has always counted is the story and the skill with which it is told."
~Michael Eisner, CEO, Disney

How To Improve Your Conversational Skills

Here are three types of conversationalists. See if any of these descriptions fit your way of describing things and talking to people.

A You have recently spent the day with your daughter, an art history professor, in New York City. Instead of taking the train or bus, you drove to Staten Island and took the ferry. When you arrived in lower Manhattan you ate at a Greek restaurant and you had the spanakopita and your daughter had stuffed grape leaves—it was very reasonably priced, less than $20 for the two of you. Then you went to Lord and Taylor and your daughter found just the pin she was looking for and you tried on five green blouses but none were the right color. After that you took a cab uptown to the Museum of Modern Art and waited 20 minutes in line to get in because on the second floor not far from the restrooms two women were having a huge fight, swinging at each other with their handbags, and the guards couldn't control them and the police were called in and the onlookers were rooting for on or the other and it was just incredible.

B You have done very well for yourself, but you know better than to brag about it, so you let people know in a subtle way. For instance, you never say "I had to take the car in for some work," you always say "I had to take the Mercedes in for some work." When the subject of watches comes up, you say "Oh, I always buy my watches at Tiffany's because they last forever." If you are going to spend the weekend with friends you wouldn't dream of saying "I'm heading out for Long Island tonight," you would have to say "I'm going to the Hamptons for a few days." Another way you avoid actual bragging is by repeating complements you have been paid. "My secretary says she's never worked for anyone who dresses as well as I do."

C You glance at the headlines every day and never miss the 11 o'clock news. If you have time, you read a few articles in *Time* or *Newsweek* every week. You consider yourself pretty well informed and feel it is important to speak out on issues. In a conversation about the fate of business in the Far East, you might say "There will be no change in Hong Kong's status. The Chinese can't afford it. People who say things are going to change don't know what they are talking about." Or if the talk turns to the arts, you might state flatly: "I don't care what the critics said, 'The Piano' was the worst movie ever made. Nothing even comes close." You, after all, read enough to know what you are talking about, right?

Let's examine these styles.

Type A

The point of your story is that two women were actually having a fist fight in the Museum of Modern Art. Your listeners really don't care how you got there or what you ate for lunch or what you did at Lord & Taylor. Before you start to tell a story, think of WHY you are telling it and omit extraneous details. For instance, were the women old or young? Were they seriously trying to hurt each other or were they just swinging handbags? Who stopped it? Type A people get so involved in the details that they forget to concentrate on the point of the story.

Type B

You need to practice real self-restraint to avoid this pitfall. For the truth is, people (with the possible exception of real estate salesmen whose eyes start spinning with dollar signs) are not going to be impressed with what you own or where you go—if anything, they find this to be a sort of one-upmanship that is tedious. Tiffany watches last a long time? So does a Timex. Would you say "I have to take the Toyota in for some work"? Probably not. There are people who wouldn't go near the Hamptons because of the massive traffic jams and the thundering hordes on the streets. And repeating what your secretary says doesn't fool anyone—you are really saying "Look how expensive my clothes are. Look what wonderful taste I have." Learn to enjoy your possessions yourself, without having to share how expensive they are with the world. And hold on to those compliments—they are flattering and do wonders for our egos. But don't share them.

Type C

You have every right to your opinion, as long as you make sure you say it's your opinion. If you preface the statement about Hong Kong with "The things I've been reading make me think. . .". or "I'm pretty convinced that. . .". The other reason it pays to make sure people understand that you are voicing only your opinion is that sometimes there is a true expert in the crowd. Someone, say, who has just spent the last year in Hong Kong writing about the transition for the London Economist. When this happens, you look foolish. How much easier it is to say "I think" before making a pronouncement.

It takes practice and vigilance to break these habits, but it's well worth your trouble.

The "I's" Have It

One of the most important things you can learn about human nature is what I call the phenomenon of the selfish mind. The average person spends almost all his time thinking and fantasizing about his most important concern: himself. It takes only 15 percent of the brain to understand and process language. That leaves the remaining 85 percent free to daydream, solve problems, or think about what to have for dinner.

We are all tuned to the most popular radio station in the world:

WIIFM:

What's
In
It
For
Me

And that means the only way to really get someone's attention is to put yourself in their shoes and position everything you say from their point of view.

People with good social skills seem to know this instinctively. They know that to influence others, you must always appeal to their self-interest. A boring person, on the other hand, is perpetually worried about himself. A bore talks AT you. He tells you things, rather than seeking to interest and involve you in a dialogue. He is a monologist and you are expected to sit and listen while he talks nonstop about himself or his opinions.

You will never be perceived as boring if you make a conscious effort to share the floor with others and listen more than you speak. And the interesting thing is, the more you listen and the less you speak, the more support you will gain for your ideas and the more trustworthy and believable you will seem.

Without good listening skills, it is almost impossible to become successful in your career or personal life.

Six tips to help you become a better listener

1 Never forget that you have two ears and one mouth, so you can listen twice as much as you speak. For some people (too many people!), this can be very difficult. You probably know someone who is a nervous talker. When nervous talkers feel stressed or insecure, they can dominate a conversation by going on and on, allowing no interruptions and speaking faster and louder than anyone who might like to interrupt this torrent of words. If you see yourself in this description, teach yourself to speak no more than three sentences in a row without pausing to let other people respond. A good goal is to listen attentively 75 percent of the time and talk no more than 25 percent.

2   Take five. After the other person stops talking, count to five before you say a word. This has three benefits: first, you give your brain the opportunity to absorb what was said and formulate an intelligent reply or question; second, you show the person who was speaking that what they said was worthy of consideration; third, you avoid interrupting the other person who may have paused only to gather his thoughts.

3   Always ask at least one clarifying question before responding with your own point of view. Some good clarifiers are "How so?" or "Can you elaborate?" Many people worry that they do not express themselves clearly. By asking for clarification, you give them an opportunity to rephrase their thoughts and say exactly what they mean. They will appreciate the courtesy.

4   Tell them what you think you heard. When you are absolutely sure the other person has finished, say: "If I understand you correctly. . ." and then paraphrase everything you think he said. The person will be flattered that you gave him your undivided attention and will correct any misunderstandings.

5 Don't judge or give advice unless specifically asked. Show your empathy by murmuring phrases such as "I understand how you feel," or "If I were you I would feel exactly the same way."

6 Look directly at the person who is speaking. Notice his hair, eyes, and face. Smile and nod as he speaks.

Broadcasters Tip
Make it relevant

Your audience will tune you out if you can't show them exactly how your message is relevant to them. When you speak, use specific examples that relate to the listener.

Selling Yourself, As Well As Your Product

To become a great salesperson, to persuade and influence others, and to get people to support your point of view, you need to learn as much as you can about your target audience: hopes, dreams, wishes, fears, needs, wants, and desires.

The best way to do this is to ask the right questions. As you know, people never seem to tire of talking about themselves. Everyone thinks he is an expert at something, and that means there is at least one topic he will hold forth on forever. Find out what that is, get him started, and he will think YOU are the most interesting person in the world. Sound strange? Consider the following true story as told by marketing expert Jay Abraham at one of his seminars.

Jay met a stranger in a hotel lounge late one night. They struck up a conversation. Being a curious type, he asked the stranger about his profession. The stranger kept talking, and Jay, a good listener, drew the man out with a series of thoughtful questions. As the man continued to talk, Jay did nothing but ask questions. When Jay, having revealed nothing about himself, finally excused himself to go to bed, the stranger shook his hand warmly and said "Sir, you are clearly the most fascinating man I have ever met!"

Here is what I learned from that story.

There are two kinds of questions, closed and open-ended. Closed questions can be answered with a yes or no. They are worthless for getting to know people, but they are good for closing a sale or forcing a person to take a position.

Open-ended questions are those you use to get to know someone. Like a good newspaper lead, they include the answers to who, what, where, when, and why. For instance, "What kind of work do you do?" "When did you get into that profession?" "Where did you grow up?" As British Prime Minister Benjamin Disraeli once said, "Talk to people about themselves and they will listen for hours." A famous society beauty, known for her ability to captivate men, reportedly told her daughter: "Ask a man about his childhood, listen politely, and he will be devastated by your amazing intelligence and quick wit."

Of course, the downside to this drawing-out is that you get stuck with this person and his autobiographical impulse until you are ready to do anything to get away. At any gathering where there is food you can always say, "You must excuse me—I'm ravenous and that food looks wonderful." Another exit line that works at big gatherings is "Please excuse me—there's Sandra Bullock and I haven't had a chance to return her calls. I've got to apologize." And of course what works anytime, anywhere is "Do excuse me—I must find the bathroom."

In addition to being good listeners, the best talkers look at things in ways that are different, perhaps slightly skewed. They have unexpected views on familiar subjects. They can talk about a wide range of issues beyond their daily lives. One way to broaden your interest and become a better conversationalist is to make sure you read at least one magazine a week that is outside your usual area of interest. And be sure to read a metropolitan newspaper every day. For instance, a woman who reads *People* or *Cosmopolitan* on a regular basis, might try *Fortune* or *Newsweek*. A man who is addicted to *Sports Illustrated* should try *The New Yorker* or *Vanity Fair.*

Broadcaster's Tip
To be interesting, be interested

The most interesting people are enthusiastic about their lives and insatiably curious about others. They have the ability to empathize. They have a sense of humor, especially about themselves. They have a unique way of expressing themselves, be it dramatic, emotional or particularly logical. Above all, they have clearly defined personalities with strong points of view on almost everything, and they are not afraid to express themselves.

You Must Remember This . . .

√   That it's a mistake to try too hard to be funny. You will find plenty of good material just by absorbing the absurdities of the world around you.

√   That you could improve your joke-telling ability by studying the technique of your favorite stand-up comic.

√   That the world won't come to an end if no one laughs at your jokes—dust yourself off and try again.

√   That to be perceived as interesting, you must be sincerely interested in others. To draw people out, ask open-ended questions.

√   That you must listen three times as much as you speak. Never speak more than three sentences without pausing to let the other person contribute.

√   That you can expand your field of knowledge by reading at least one magazine a week that is outside your normal area of interest.

10

State Your Case Effectively

Have you ever noticed how some people seem to have a knack for communicating with others? They know how to say the right thing at just the right time. They seem to have a baffling ability to charmingly disarm even the most hostile or intimidating person with nothing more than a few choice words. These people seem to have a mysterious psychological advantage that allows them to make their arguments so persuasive they get whatever it is they are after.

For some people, this outstanding ability to communicate is an intuitive skill—a gift of diplomacy they were born with. But for the rest of us, it is something we need to learn if we are to maximize our potential.

Psychological researchers have found that when it comes to predicting success, your brain power matters much less than your emotional power. They call this emotional intelligence, or EQ—your Emotional Quotient.

Contrary to what was commonly believed, the kind of intelligence measured by IQ tests is responsible for only 20 percent of your ability to succeed. The true measure of your success is measured by your ability to understand your own feelings and express empathy for the feelings of others—your EQ.

These findings were confirmed by managers at Bell Laboratories, one of the nation's most prestigious research labs. At Bell Labs, the top performers were not the socially awkward geniuses who spent time alone hunched over computers. Instead, the team members who were promoted had a special ability to communicate and collaborate, regardless of brain power. They were all people with high EQs.

Researchers from the Center for Creative Leadership studied de-railed executives in the United States and abroad; here, too, they found that executives failed more because of emotional flaws than because of issues related to performance.

The communications skills that comprise EQ include empathy, graciousness, and the ability to "read" other people in social situations. A high EQ is not important just for getting along with co-workers. EQ is essential for anyone wanting to compete in today's market. Customers are telling businesses that they could not care less about whether the employees they deal with have degrees from a prestigious business school—all they care about is being listened to, understood, and treated with respect. One thing is certain: if your customers do not get the kind of respectful treatment they expect, they will take their business elsewhere.

One of the major goals of this book is to help you increase your EQ by communicating in ways that convey respect and understanding. IQ is commonly thought to be a fixed measurement resulting from factors outside your control, such as genetics and social conditioning. EQ is a measurement of the way you relate to others. While you may or may not be able to increase your IQ, anyone can raise his EQ by learning a few simple communication techniques.

High EQ people communicate in a three-stage process.

- In Stage One, they establish empathy, acknowledge emotions, respond to excitement, and ask questions to determine if their timing is right before proceeding.

- In Stage Two, they create a sense of psychological obligation, listen for "hot buttons," and keep checking for a willingness to listen.

- In Stage Three, they measure their impact.

Let's examine these three stages.

Stage One

The first part of Stage One is to establish empathy. The ability to empathize is vital for anyone who wants to communicate with understanding and compassion. Empathy is the ability to communicate that you really understand the other person's problems, feelings, and points of view. Unfortunately, empathy is a very scarce commodity—the good news is that empathy is a skill that can be learned and improved through practice.

To be more empathic, you have to make a simple mental shift. This is accomplished by taking a moment to ask yourself how you would think and feel if you were in the other person's shoes. Training yourself to empathize is one of the habits Stephen Covey refers to in his book *Seven Habits of Highly Effective People*. In Covey's words, seek first to understand, before you seek to be understood.

In the last chapter, I mentioned that the most listened-to radio station in the world is WIIFM—What's In It For Me. But if you tune to radio station What's In It For YOU (YOU being the other person), you will notice that the quality of your communication makes a radical shift. You will gain the trust of others. People will be more likely to confide in you. It will be easier for others to clarify their ideas, and in turn they will be more empathic with you.

Throughout the empathy-building process, let others know that you recognize how they feel. When someone seems to be upset, say (in a soft voice), "You seem upset. What's the matter?" When a person appears irritated or angry, say "You don't seem like yourself—tell me what's wrong." If the person is willing to open up to you (and not all people will be), don't offer advice or try to fix the problem, just say "I can certainly understand how you are feeling." Responding in this way may encourage the person to talk it out and work through anger or nervousness. By being a non-judgmental listener, you will be most able to help the other person—they, in turn, will find you more interesting.

Another way to gain the friendship and trust of others is to share their enthusiasm and joy. Imagine how you would feel if you came home excited that you had won a new account and were greeted by your spouse with a bored "That's nice, honey." But notice the difference if you were greeted with "That's great—tell me about it!" Your spouse is using a tone of voice that matches your excitement.

People with a high EQ are extremely skilled at "reading" other people. One of the ways they do this is with a test-question technique. Have you ever needed to ask a moody person for something? With people like that, timing is everything. If you get them at a bad time, they will not be receptive and any answer will be NO. The test-question technique is a great way to test moods.

Here's how it works. Imagine you want to ask your mercurial boss for a raise. You obviously cannot just come out and ask him what kind of a mood he is in. Instead, try asking an innocent question about an unrelated event, such as the weather. If you say "Isn't this a glorious day?" and get a muttered response, you will know it's a good idea to postpone your request.

Stage Two

Once you have built a bridge of empathy to the other person, you are ready to go on to Stage Two and create a sense of psychological obligation. This is not a diabolical plan—it's a tried and true method for getting others to treat you with respect and kindness.

There is no magic formula—all you have to do is be the first to extend the same courtesy to them. Do you want to be helped? Then help someone first. Do you want your ideas to be heard? Then listen attentively to the ideas of others. Do you want your mistakes to be forgiven? Then forgive and forget the mistakes of others.

Practicing these courteous acts is more than just good moral conduct. It actually has the psychological effect of obliging others to treat you in kind. The interesting thing about psychological obligation is that it is cumulative. If you practice courteous acts without concern for whether or not they will be returned by a specific individual, the positive effect will spread like an aura around you, improving the way you are treated in general—and raising your EQ,

Another trait of high EQs is listening for "hot buttons." A hot button is a topic that motivates the other to pay attention to what you have to say. Some typical hot buttons are money, respect, security, happiness. But not everyone responds to the same hot buttons. The best way to find the strongest hot button for a particular person is to listen carefully and notice the recurring themes in his conversation—the things he likes to talk about.

For example, if you have a customer who repeatedly talks about boating, don't just tell him he will like your product; show him how your product or service will make him so much money he will be able to buy that new sailboat he has had his eye on.

Broadcaster's Tip
How to keep 'em tuned in
Audience researcher Frank Magid found that people will always listen to topics that pertain to their "health, heart and pocketbook."

Another key characteristic of high EQs is their ability to read social situations. One of the ways they do this in conversation is by checking on whether or not the other person is willing to listen. There are three cues that will give you an idea on how open a person is to your ideas. The first is uncertainty; the second is partial approval; the third is asking for details.

You will know your prospect is open to your ideas if he seems uncertain about his own. You can spot that uncertainty if he prefaces his ideas with "maybe" or "I'm not sure, but . . .".

If your prospect expresses partial approval—agreeing with some of your points, disagreeing with others—you will know he is listening and can continue to try to win him over.

If you get asked for more details, you'll know you are close to winning him over. A disinterested, or uninterested, person would not ask questions and would cut you off before you could respond.

Stage Three

Stage Three, gauging your impact, can be as simple as asking the other person if he is interested in your topic. For instance, if you have been talking about the Internet, ask "What do you think about the worldwide web?" If his answer is "I don't know, I guess it's okay," it's time to move on to something else.

Persuasion

Persuasiveness is often referred to as an art. But it can be boiled down to a three-step process that can be learned and perfected with practice.

- Step I - Setting the stage

- Step II - Presenting your case

- Step III - The summary

Step I - Setting The Stage

You cannot foster understanding with someone who is not willing to listen. You can vastly improve your chances of being persuasive if you create a mood that is open, supportive, and free of criticism. You can do this easily by using the soft, tender tone of voice you learned earlier in the book. Let your listener know that throughout the discussion you will not criticize and that you will remain open to what he has to say. If you take exception to anything he says, or act offended, he will only become more entrenched in his point of view and less likely to see yours.

A common tendency, when we are arguing emotionally about something that is truly important to us, is to make the other person feel as if you are trying to overpower him or force your ideas down his throat. You will never gain anything under these conditions.

A more effective strategy is to act as if the acceptance of your ideas is not that important to you, even though you may be gnashing your teeth silently. You must act as though it is a minor point you wanted to mention. This will take some practice if your idea is something that means a lot to you. But I guarantee that the self-control it takes to use this technique will be more than worth it in the long run. Another important part of setting the stage is breaking your listener's preoccupation. Have you ever tried to discuss an important matter with someone whose mind was a million miles away? He might seem unusually quiet or keep glancing away while you are talking. You could give up, go away, and hope for the best next time, but that means you have wasted your time and lost control of the situation. Instead, try this technique to turn bad timing into good and create the receptivity you need.

Address the situation directly by saying, "You seem to have a lot on your mind. Is something bothering you?" This will encourage the person to open up and get his worries off his chest. Once he does that, you have built trust and created an open climate—and it is the perfect time to begin your discussion. If he is not forthcoming, you would be wise to wait for another time to make your pitch.

Because most of us are self-involved—distracted by our own thoughts and responsibilities—you sometimes need to jump through hoops to get another person's attention. When this happens, your voice is one of your most effective attention-grabbing tools.

Keep the rhythm of your speech staccato and crisp. Use lots of body language. Speak distinctly and slightly louder than usual. This is no time to be vague. Create an attention-grabbing headline to open your conversation, just as you would in a sales letter. "Boss, I have just come up with a way to increase our profits by 236 percent—can I tell you about it?"

Have you ever tried to have a logical conversation with someone who was in an excited, emotional state? Whether the emotion is frustration, anger, fear, or even elation, the intensity of the feeling has captured his full attention and prevents him from listening rationally to what you have to say. He might seem combative, defensive, secretive or overbearing, but no matter what emotion is being expressed, you must clear away these emotions that are standing in the way of a rational discussion.

When someone gets emotional, do not respond in kind. Instead, address the emotion and get it out in the open. If a person seems argumentative, say, "You sound angry. Tell me what happened." If the person does begin to talk, show your empathy by saying that you understand the feeling and would feel the same way yourself under those conditions. To get through to an emotional person, you must deal with the emotion, let the feelings get talked out, before you can even begin to state your case. The best way to do this is through a process called mirroring.

Normally you can tell when a person is in an emotional state just by looking at him. Over the phone, you can almost always tell by the tone of voice. Comment on what you see or hear by mirroring the emotion back to the person. "You seem really happy today," or "You sound upset," or "You sound angry." This directs the person to the emotion and he could begin to talk about what happened and why he is feeling the way he is. Encourage him to continue until you sense that his feelings are fully vented and he has said everything he has to say. Then, as emotions clear away, he will be able to think more clearly. And he will be more willing and able to listen rationally to your point of view.

The final component of setting the stage is to gather information. You do this by asking questions to get the information you need to construct your argument. The trick, though, is to ask your questions without annoying or offending the other person.

Here are three types of questions that will help you do this.

1   Fact-finding questions. Journalists refer to these as
    the five Ws—who, what, where, when, and why.

The answers to these questions provide essential background information that will help you understand the opposing viewpoint.

2 The supposition. Here you force the other person to evaluate his position by asking him how his idea would work under various circumstances. If you were a technical director trying to persuade your conservative CEO to invest more money in research and development, you might ask: "Suppose our competition began investing heavily in R&D and came up with a product improvement that allowed them to increase market share by 25 percent?" Suppositions force the other person to evaluate his ideas from a broader perspective.

3 The justifier. Use these when someone makes a general statement such as "Inflation will be worse next year." With a general statement like that, it is certainly reasonable to ask for some supporting data, so you might ask what makes him say that or why does he think so?

Step II - Presenting Your Case

Once you have set the stage, it's time to present your case. As you do, the other person is sure to raise objections. Here are three effective ways to deal with this.

First, repeat the objection. This is a deceptively simple but powerful persuasion technique. It works especially well in a stalemate. All you do is repeat the person's comments back to him and pause while he reflects on his own words. By doing this, you are mirroring his thoughts and emotions back to him. This forces him to evaluate objectively what he said. If his words sound unreasonable, it is much easier for him to say that you have misinterpreted his idea, rather than admit it sounds unworkable. You are giving him the opportunity to change his opinion without losing face.

Let's say Mary wants to persuade John that they should spend their vacation in Mexico. John refuses, saying "Absolutely not. Everyone who goes to Mexico gets sick from the water." Mary responds with "Everyone gets sick from the water?" John thinks for a minute and says, "Well, not everyone. But going there still makes me nervous."

Now John has softened his position, leaving an opening for Mary to tell him about the special Mexican vacation package she found for three nights in a luxurious five-star hotel, right on the beach. At this point, John might say, "Oh, you didn't mention a great deal at a five-star hotel—that's another story."

Any time you are trying to prove a point or persuade someone to do something, you are bound to encounter resistance and objections. The worst thing to do is to try and match the objections with equal force. We tend to think that if we argue longer or louder we will eventually overpower the other person and force him to change his mind. Wrong—by doing this, you might cause the other person to give up and walk away, but you won't convince him of your point of view.

A much more effective tactic is to uncover and clarify each objection so you can understand and deal with them one at a time. Get the person to talk at length about his objections by asking open-ended questions as to who, what, where, when, and why. This lifts the resistance out of the realm of a hard-line negative stance and gives you the information you need to form a logical rebuttal to each point.

Melanie, age 18, wanted to borrow the family car on a Saturday night. She was met with a resounding NO from her mother. This situation could have resulted in a nasty, door-slamming argument, in which the mother would certainly not have been persuaded to give Melanie the keys and both mother and daughter would have retreated to their respective rooms, irritated and upset.

But Melanie used a different approach. She calmly asked her mother why she felt the way she did. Her mother told her about a neighbor's son who had just been injured in a car accident while driving drunk. Melanie was able to assure her mother that she would never drink and drive. She promised to call her mother when she reached her destination. The mother agreed to lend Melanie the car and they negotiated a reasonable time when she should be back home.

Sometimes the person you are trying to convince will try to sidetrack you while you are in the middle of your pitch. Just as you are getting into it, he changes the subject and tries to steer the conversation to some unrelated issue of his own. The best way to deal with this is to acknowledge his point, but remain firm about sticking to YOUR point right now. It is often helpful to preface this with a statement such as "That's a very valid point, but it will take some time to address it, so let's finish discussing my proposal first."

Step III - The Summary

When you have used all these methods to build your persuasive argument, you are ready for Step III, the summary. As you summarize your facts and your conclusions, both you and your listener have one more chance to clarify any misunderstanding. But here is an important tip: After summarizing your point of view, be sure also to summarize the points of disagreement. By doing this, you show respect and prove that you have listened carefully to his objections. As you re-cap his objections, you can also add how you propose to solve your differences.

Some excellent questions to ask during the summary are: Have I made everything clear? Have I answered all your questions? Is there anything you disagree with that you would like to discuss further?

Before you go to sleep tonight, take a moment to review these steps in the persuasion process. If you have a sale to make or a boss to convince tomorrow, it will be time well spent.

You Must Remember This . . .

√   That two factors play an important part in your success—your IQ and your EQ. And it's been substantiated that your EQ (Emotional Quotient) is the more important of the two.

√   That high EQ people communicate in a three-stage process—establishing empathy, creating a sense of psychological obligation, and measuring their impact.

√   That your voice is one of your most effective tools in persuasion, which also has three elements to it: setting the stage, presenting your argument, or pitch, and summarizing.

11

The 26 Biggest Telephone "Turn-Offs" And How To Avoid Them

This chapter is for anyone who would like to brush up on phone etiquette. It's a great training aid for anyone who answers your phone and a handy check list for teens about to enter the work place. But the information is this chapter is not only for neophytes. I've heard even seasoned business professionals do some of the telephone "don'ts" outlined below. If you spend more than five minutes a day on the phone, take a moment to scan this list to make sure you are not inadvertently making any of these common telephone mistakes.

Telephone Turn-Off #1
Cradling the receiver between your ear and your shoulder

It's tempting to cradle the receiver in order to keep both hands free to write or refer to papers while you speak, but here's why you shouldn't. It forces your chin against your chest, constricting your voice and giving you that muffled "I'm calling for the ransom money" sound. Cradling the phone also puts enormous strain on the upper part of your spine, which can literally give you a pain in the neck and send you to the chiropractor! Do yourself and your voice a favor: buy the highest quality headset you can afford.

Telephone Turn-Off #2
The Speakerphone

Try not to use a speakerphone unless absolutely necessary. I believe they are rude because the other party must strain to hear you. Speakerphone technology can also make you sound as if you are calling from the rest room—not good for a business call. In a noisy environment, the speakerphone can pick up distracting office noises, which may interfere with the conversation. And because of the technology, any emotion or warmth in the voice is lost. You lose the ability to pick up or transmit subtle emotional cues.

I believe there are only three times one should use a speakerphone:

- While waiting on hold.

- When speaking to computer tech-support (so both hands are free to use your computer while they talk to you)

- When there is more than one person in the room who needs to speak.

Telephone Turn-Off #3
A Grouchy Voice

If you smile when you dial, you will never sound grouchy. It's the fastest and easiest way to sound warm and friendly. In fact, this technique is so powerful, it even works when you are in a bad mood! But to have a genuine smile in your voice, the smile on your face must be visible. Keep a mirror by your phone. When you can see a nice big grin in the mirror, you can be sure the person you are calling will hear the smile in your voice.

Telephone Turn-Off #4
Sloppy Body Language

Many people think that because the person they are speaking to can't see them it's okay to relax their professional demeanor. You know what I mean ... lean way back in the chair... slouch, put your feet up on your desk, scratch your .... uh ... whatever. Well, they might not be able to see you. But they can definitely hear it in your voice.

When making business or professional calls, sit as if you were actually face to face with the person you are calling. Gesture and imagine you are making eye contact in your mind. If you have never met them, try to imagine what they look like based on the sound of their voice.

Broadcasters Tip
Smile at the one you love

Some broadcasters keep a photo of a loved one by their microphone. They find they sound more focused, warm and friendly if they make eye contact with a picture of someone they love during their broadcasts.

Telephone Turn-Off #5
Verbal viruses

We learned about these in an earlier chapter. To avoid them, tape record a days worth of phone calls (your side of the conversation only. Tape recording another person without their consent is illegal) By doing so you will hear how you really sound to others. You'll notice the non-words and verbal fillers you use (such as mm, like, sort of, you know), how much you listen, and whether there are any shifts in your energy level throughout the day. Do you sound great in the morning but exhausted by day's end?

Make a point of asking more questions and spending more time listening to what others have to say. Remember: the most successful salespeople speak no more than 25% of the time.

If you are truly committed to having a million dollar telephone voice, recording and transcribing a day's worth of calls is the single best way to improve the way you sound.

Telephone Turn-Off #6
Doing paperwork (or other tasks) while speaking on the phone

You'll get distracted and be tempted to tune out. As a rule of thumb, while on the phone, don't do anything you wouldn't do if you were speaking to the person face to face. Giving phone calls less than your full attention is the same as turning your back during a conversation. The person you are speaking to can hear it in your voice. To help accomplish this, keep distracting piles of paper out of sight and as far away from the phone as possible.

Telephone Turn-Off #7
Answering the phone on the first ring

When the phone rings, all too often we drop what we are doing, grab the receiver and answer in a harried tone of voice. This can make you sound brusque and unfriendly and is not very welcoming to the person who is calling. Instead, let the phone ring once, take a deep breath, compose yourself, and smile before you pick up the receiver and greet the caller. You'll be amazed at how much better you'll sound.

Telephone Turn-Off #8
Answering the phone when you are upset, or truly do not wish to be disturbed

Have you ever had the unpleasant experience of calling someone at work or at home and catching them at a bad moment? These moments happen to all of us. But in this day and age when everyone has access to answering machines and voicemail, I'm always amazed that people answer their phone in the middle of an argument, while half asleep, or while rushing to meet a deadline. It's better to let technology take over than risk giving the caller a bad impression

Telephone Turn-Off #9
Not saying your name *last*

When someone other than the person you are calling answers the phone, ask first for the name of the person you wish to speak with before giving your name. The person who answers the phone is listening for the name of the person to whom they must route the call. If you give your name last they'll be less likely to forget it.

Telephone Turn-Off #10
Not practicing your opening remarks

The first 12 seconds of any call are the most important. That's all it takes for someone to form a lasting first impression about who you are and what you have to offer. When making important calls, you'll increase your chances of success by practicing aloud the tone and content of your opening until it's as effective as can be. Memorize your opening remarks and practice into a tape recorder. Don't make the call until you are confident you sound smooth and spontaneous. Whatever you do, don't read from a script!

Telephone Turn-Off #11
Not stating the purpose of your call up front

You'll put busy people at ease if you start your call with a clear agenda. For example: "Ms. Jones, there are two reasons for my call today..." This helps the person you are calling pay attention and eliminates any fears that you will be taking an unlimited chunk of their time.

Telephone Turn-Off #12
Not using verbal nods

To make people comfortable and encourage them to continue speaking, make sure you use plenty of verbal nods in your speech. Verbal nods are phrases like: "I see," "good," "Go on," "really!" "that's interesting," "uh, huh." Most people use them unconsciously, but occasionally you'll run across someone who doesn't. I once had a friend who did not use verbal nods. His telephone silence made me wonder if he had fallen asleep on the other end of the phone.

Telephone Turn-Off #13
Not listening!

When we can't see body language, it can be hard to know how we are being received. But we can learn to listen for and analyze the subtle verbal nods (see above) people give us to know how we're doing.

Sales psychology experts say there are three stages of verbal nods. In stage one, the verbal nods are slow and deliberate. The person is warming up to what you are saying. In stage two, the verbal nods become faster. The person is becoming more excited and interested. But if the verbal nods become extremely fast, such as a quick succession of rapid fire "Uh huh, uh huh, uh huh's" you're in stage three and it's time to back off. The person is trying to tell you to quit talking and give him a chance to speak.

Telephone Turn-Off #14
Not using the callers name when receiving a transferred call

Welcome the caller by using their name and let them know you'll be happy to help them with the information they need.

Telephone Turn-Off #15
Not getting their name and contact information right away

If they are calling in response to an ad, getting their name, number and address before you give them information will assure that you get the caller tracking information you need for your database. Getting their name and number up front also assures that you can call them back if you get disconnected.

Telephone Turn-Off #16
Playing music or the radio in the background

Playing music in the background while at work can hinder your ability to concentrate on what callers are saying and can be distracting. The telephone receiver might pick up the background music, which will make it difficult for the caller to hear you.

Telephone Turn-Off #17
Not giving callers the name of the person you are transferring them to and the reason why

Never transfer a caller without telling them why. By giving them the name and title of a person who can help them, you'll help diffuse their impatience.

Telephone Turn-Off #18
Not letting the caller hang up first

When I'm calling a business for information the most important questions tend to pop into my head right as I am hanging up the phone. I shout into the receiver... "Wait! One more thing!" But it's usually too late. Wouldn't it be nice if more customer service reps waited to see if scatter brained people like me had one last question?

Telephone Turn-Off #19
Using phrases that can be perceived as abrupt or even rude

Here is a list of some common abrupt phrases and some suggested replacements:

Avoid	Replace with
"Who's calling"	"May I tell him/her who's calling please?"
"What company are you with" "Who are you representing"	"Is there something I (or other assistant) can help you with?
"He/she is in a meeting"	"He/she is not available. I'm (your name), his/her assistant. May I help you?"

Telephone Turn-Off #20
Not letting prospects, clients or customers, remain in control

Never tell them what they need to do, have to do or must do. Instead say: "May I make a suggestion..." or "With your permission..."

Telephone Turn-Off #21
Making the conversation all about you

Don't tell callers what *you* want or what *you'd* like to do. They could care less! Don't say "You don't understand *me*." Instead say: "From what you just said I'm not sure if I expressed myself clearly..."

Telephone Turn-Off #22
Using the words: "Can't," or "That's impossible."

It frustrates callers. Instead say: "That may be difficult" or "That may not be feasible."

Telephone Turn-Off #23
Saying you don't know the answer to a question

Instead, find someone who does know! Say to the caller: "I'll be happy to look into that for you and get right back to you with an answer."

Telephone Turn-Off #24
Putting people on hold without telling them why

Always try to help a caller before putting them on hold. If you must put them on hold, ask for their permission to do so and tell them why. Never leave someone on hold for more than twenty seconds without coming back to see if they want to continue holding or wish to leave a message.

Telephone Turn-Off #25
Taking incomplete messages

Always repeat the name, address and company name and ask the caller to spell it. To confirm the telephone number, repeat it back to the caller.

Telephone turnoff #26
Using the phrase "I'll be honest with you."

It implies you may have lied in the past. Better: "To be perfectly frank."

You Must Remember This . . .

√ That you should avoid cradling the receiver between your ear and your shoulder. It forces your chin against your chest, constricting your voice and giving you a muffled sound.

√ That you should invest in the highest quality head-set you can afford.

√ That you should keep a mirror and/or a picture of a loved one by your desk, and smile before you dial.

√ That you shouldn't let yourself be distracted while on the phone. People can hear it in your voice!

√ That you should always be courteous to clients and prospects by paying attention to their concerns, by not keeping them on hold for more than 20 seconds, and by always letting them know you will do your best to get their questions answered promptly.

12

How To Leave Voicemail Messages
That Get Returned
(And Get Results!)

Funny thing about voicemail. We love it when it's our own but hate it when it belongs to someone else. I don't know about you, but when someone doesn't return my messages, I imagine they are gloating behind my back, laughing demonically as they push the delete button to send me to into oblivion.

Actually, I doubt if most people are this cold. But what's so frustrating about voicemail is it gives the decision maker the opportunity to reject you before you even get a chance to talk to them! If you're starting to feel like a failure because people won't return your messages, here's what to do.

I believe most messages do not get returned because people are overwhelmed. Many of us move through our work day in a state that ranges from mild panic to deep despair. To get returned, a message must be so compelling that it wins out over all the other things vying for the recipient's attention. Yet, many messages do not even come close to addressing the specific needs, desires, wants, and concerns of the person being called.

There's the sales rep who leaves a message saying she would like to stop by and talk with you about advertising in her paper. Yeah right. Like you've got nothing better to do. The copier company calling to sell you toner. Toner? There are six boxes stacked in the closet. Or the person you've never heard of asking you to call him back. You don't mean to be rude but apparently these people assume you're just sitting around with nothing else to do!

To help solve this problem, I asked some successful business people I know to share their best voicemail techniques. I cannot guarantee that any of these methods will give you a 100% call back ratio, but they will definitely help improve your odds. Test them out and you'll quickly discover the ones that work best for you.

1   **Leave 'em guessing**
    Curiosity is a powerful motivator. Try leaving messages with nothing more than your name and number. Do not say why you are calling. My own sales staff found that this one simple technique increased their call back ratio by 40%! Busy people calling in for messages from the road will also appreciate your brevity.

2   **The "Pains" technique**
    This is an excellent technique to use as a follow up to a sales presentation. In your initial meeting with the prospect ask probing questions to determine "where it hurts." Make a list of these "pains" and how your product or service can provide specific relief for each concern. Each time you leave a

follow up message, mention one of your prospect's "pains" and hint at how you can provide relief. Refer to a different problem each time you call. For example:

Message #1: "Ms. Jones, this is Susan Berkley from Berkley Productions at 201-541-8595. I'm calling to offer some solutions as to how our voice recording services can give you a more professional sounding voice mail system and get rid of that annoying recorded voice you told me about that was bothering the company president. My number again is…."

Message #2: Ms. Jones, this is Susan Berkley from Berkley Productions at 201-541-8595. I'm calling with a few solutions to help you reduce those customer complaints about getting lost in your voicemail system that you spoke about in our last meeting. My number again is…"

Message #3: Ms. Jones, this is Susan Berkley from Berkley Productions at 201-541-8595. I'm calling with an easy, cost effective way to help you provide information to your Spanish and Vietnamese speaking customers. You seemed concerned about this in our last meeting and I wanted to discuss some of the ways we help our customers meet this challenge. My number again is…"

3   **Tell them you are calling from corporate headquarters**

It adds credibility, especially if you are a

small or home based business! "Hello, this is Susan Berkley with Berkley Productions corporate headquarters. The reason for the call is..."

4   **Leave your first *and* last name**
Using only your first name can cause confusion "Steve who? I know five guys named Steve!"

5   **Eliminate minimizers from your speech**
Examples: "I'm *only* calling to follow up on yesterdays meeting." "Nothing important. *Just* a follow up call to yesterday's meeting." "*Merely* a little reminder about how our widget can help build your business." These minimizers diminish the impact of your message.

6   **Don't sell anything in the message**
Because we are constantly bombarded with advertising, most people have developed a strong sales resistance. If you sell in your voicemail, the people you are calling will reject you unless you happen to catch them at a moment when they have a passionate desire or need for your product.

7   **Make the benefits contingent on speaking with you**
"This is Susan Berkley from XYZ distribu-

tors. We have just purchased a number of widgets from a company that went out of business and have priced the stock at a deep discount for fast liquidation. To determine if they are the right size and color for your needs, we need to talk. Call me at..."

8 Speak more slowly and clearly than normal

Don't slur or run your words together. The person you are calling might become annoyed if you make them replay the message because they did not understand it.

9 Spell your name if it is difficult, unusual or of foreign origin

Sometimes an unusual name is easier to remember than a name that is more common. The listener has to work harder to understand it and is more likely to remember you because he made that extra effort. Reinforce this phenomenon by saying your name clearly and spelling it slowly when you leave your message. An unusual name can make you stand out from the crowd and invites ice-breaking chit chat about the name's origin.

10 Sound like a winner by speaking with energy, enthusiasm and confidence

Sit up straight or stand when you leave voicemail. Smile as you speak. Visualize yourself as confident and strong. Use hand gestures and powerful body language. If possible, check your energy level by listening to your message before sending it

11   Leave your phone number twice: once at the beginning of your message and once at the end

If your callback number is only at the end of the message and the listenner misses it the first time through, he has to listen to the entire message again to get it.

12   Call again and offer some useful information:

"I've been thinking about you situation and have a solution that might work. I'd like to share it with you. Please call me at ...." Do not leave the solution in the message. Use it as bait to get them to call you back. Caution: do not use this technique unless you actually have something useful to share with the prospect when they call!

13   Fax your prospect a giant message slip

Take a standard "While you were out" phone message slip, fill it out with your message, enlarge it on the copier and fax it to your prospect. "While You Were Out ... Melissa Smith called Re: A few ideas to help you save big on your taxes."

14 When all else fails, politely threaten to "close their file"

Making sure there is nothing hostile or impatient in your tone of voice, leave a polite message that goes something like this: "Mr. Smith, I've been attempting to reach you for several weeks now regarding the proposal you asked us to send on January 24th. But I have not received a call back. I don't want to bug you or clog your voice mail with unwanted messages, so would you please call me back and let me know if you would like me to close your file?" It is almost humorous how quickly this message has gotten people to call us back. People like to leave their options open. Nobody likes to be terminated.

15 Make sure *your* outgoing voicemail message sounds as professional as possible

When people call your voicemail do you sound welcoming, honest, energetic and sincere or do you sound angry, bored or half asleep? Here are several steps to follow to put your "best voice" forward.

• **Script** your message. Writing it out will help you say exactly what you need to say: nothing more, nothing less. You'll also be less likely to flub when reading from a script. And you'll find it easier to control your pacing and tone when you've got something written to practice.

- **Practice** your message before you record it. Repeat it out loud to become familiar with the words.

- **Stand** while recording your message. This will add energy and vitality to your voice.

- **Smile** while recording your message. A smile makes your voice sound warm and friendly.

- **Get feedback** from at least 3 friends or colleagues. Does your message sound as good as it could? If not, re-record!

- **Don't leave flubs** or stumbles on your outgoing message. I am amazed at how many people do this, especially when re-recording is so easy to do!

- **Customize** your message daily. If possible, let people know if you are in or out of the office and when you will be likely to call them back.

- **Include your USP** in your message. Your USP is your unique selling proposition, a phrase that articulates a key benefit to your customer. Boil the USP down to a brief phrase and use it in your outgoing message. For example: "Thank you for calling XYZ language school. We guarantee that you'll start speaking the language of your choice in 30 days or less or your money back. Leave your name and number at the tone and we'll

get back to you as soon as we get your
message…"

You Must Remember This . . .

√   That to get returned, a message must be so
compelling that it wins out over all the other
things vying for the recipient's attention.

√   That effective voicemail messages,
address the specific needs,desires, wants,
and concerns of the person being called.

√   That you'll improve you chances of a call
back if you're clear and sound like a winner.

√   That sometimes less is more. Leaving only a
name and number may increase callbacks.

√   That your outgoing message is important
too! Record it with care.

13

How To Keep From Losing Your Voice
(Even When Everyone Around You
Is Sneezing And Coughing
In Your Face)

If you've ever been concerned about the health of your voice, the information in this chapter is for you. To get the low-down on proper voice care, I interviewed Dr. Wallace Rubin, a top Ear, Nose and Throat doctor. Dr. Rubin is a clinical professor of Otorhinolaryngology and Bio-Communication at Louisiana State University School of Medicine. He also has a private practice in New Orleans where he treats professional opera singers and other performers. Here's what I learned from Dr. Rubin.

What Causes Laryngitis?

Laryngitis results from a swelling of the mucus membrane over the vocal chords. It is usually caused by a bacterial or viral infection or by an allergy affecting the respiratory tree. The respiratory tree has mucus lining that Dr. Rubin compares to a wall-to-wall carpet running through a house. The lining begins at the nose and sinuses and continues past the voice box into the lungs. This lining contains protective chemicals that usually prevent infections in the nose, sinus, or lungs from spreading to other parts of the respiratory tree. But sometimes the protective chemicals don't work and an infection in the lungs or nose attacks the voice box.

In the wintertime, the warm, heated air we breathe dries out the mucus membranes and the protective chemicals along the respiratory tract making us more vulnerable to infection. Therefore, we are more likely to develop laryngitis during the winter months when infections are more prevalent and heaters are turned on.

How To Lessen Your Chances Of Losing Your Voice

According to Dr. Rubin, the best thing to do is humidify your environment, especially while you sleep. Do this by turning down the heat at night and running a humidifier. But be careful about the kind of humidifier you use. Cool mist humidifiers can promote the growth of molds and yeast, causing allergies. Warm mist humidifiers are less likely to do so. Some humidifiers add ultraviolet light for further sterilization. No matter which kind of humidifier you get, be sure to clean it frequently, following the manufacturers directions. Air purifiers are also helpful in removing allergens from your environment.

If you work in a crowded office you'll be happy to know that it's difficult to catch a sore throat by using someone else's telephone. Dr. Rubin says sore throat germs are usually transmitted by airborne particles in coughs or sneezes. You can also get sick by sharing infected silverware or glasses. Washing your dishes in the dishwasher will sterilize them.

Sore Throat Rx

If you get a sore throat and your symptoms are mild, Dr.

Rubin says you can safely wait a day or two before seeing the doctor. Things should improve if you get extra rest, eat well and increase your fluid intake. If you are feeling at all under the weather, skip your regular workout session. Vigorous exercise can temporarily lower your immunity and make things worse. Dr. Rubin also advises against drinking alcohol while sick because of its dehydrating effects.

See your doctor right away if your sore throat is accompanied by a fever or if your symptoms persist or worsen after 48 hours. According to Dr. Rubin, too many doctors prescribe antibiotics over the phone without conducting the tests necessary for a proper diagnosis. The symptoms of viral and bacterial infections are often the same. In fact, what you think is a cold can actually be an allergy with a secondary infection. Once a simple blood count or smear of the nasal secretions is done, the doctor can tell immediately if the problem is bacterial, viral or allergic and prescribe the proper treatment for your problem.

Only bacterial infections respond to antibiotics. Antibiotics can cause side effects so take them only if you really need them. If your throat problems are caused by a virus, prescription medications are now available that will help build your immunity. Once the infection is addressed, your doctor may prescribe additional medications for swelling and blockage such as antihistamines, decongestants and nasal steroids. With proper treatment, many people can recover their voice in as little as 24 hours.

The next time you get a cold or allergy attack, think twice before reaching for an over-the-counter nasal spray. Dr. Rubin says those over-the-counter nasal sprays which affect the autonomic nervous system such as Neo-synephrine or Afrin, should be used only as directed on a short term basis. These sprays open clogged nasal passages by causing immediate shrinking of the mucous membranes. However, as the medication wears off, the membranes swell again. The more you use these sprays, the less the membranes shrink and the more they swell. Over time, more and more of the medication is needed to achieve the desired effect. Personally, I avoid these sprays altogether. I've found the drying effect is not good for the sound of my voice.

How To Ensure The Health Of Your Voice

1   Break the throat clearing habit. Sore throats, whether caused by allergies or infection, are often accompanied by postnasal drainage dripping on the vocal chords. When this happens, the urge to clear the throat is in-stinctual. If the situation is chronic, throat clearing can become habitual, irritating the vocal chords. According to Dr. Rubin, clear-ing a sore, irritated throat is like banging a swollen arm or a leg against the wall. He encourages his patients to try and swallow instead. It can be difficult to change your habit pattern because it's a lot more pleasing to clear your throat than it is to swallow but if you can avoid the clearing reflex he says you'll get well faster.

2   Drink lots of water. At least eight glasses a day is best. You may want to drink even more in the winter to counteract the drying effects of central heating. Fluids like fresh fruit juices are also helpful, but too much black coffee or tea can be dehydrating.

3   Stay away from cigarettes. Cigarette smoke is so irritating that even non-smokers will become hoarse after a night in a smoky bar.

4   Go easy on your voice. Prolonged screaming
or yelling to an audience can stress the vocal
chords and cause swelling When speaking in
public, use a microphone whenever possible.

Allergies And The Voice

If you suffer from hay fever and are sensitive to trees, grass and
pollen, you know it. But many people don't know that food sensitivi-
ties can also cause allergic symptoms and problems with the voice. If
you are allergic to something you inhale, you will probably know it
almost immediately. But food allergies can take as long as 72 hours
to appear so you may need to see an allergist for diagnosis and
treatment.

To determine if you suffer from a food allergy, your doctor may
conduct a "provocative" food or chemical test. Certain suspicious
foods are eliminated from the diet and then re-introduced one by one
to see what happens. First, you avoid the suspected food or chemical
for a number of days. Then, you expose yourself following your
doctor's instructions on the day prior to your office visit. The most
common food allergens are milk, dairy, soy, wheat, peanut and egg.
Dr. Rubin says there is no need to suffer from allergies. Your doctor
can prescribe medication to take after you've been exposed to an
allergen to prevent attacks from occurring.

You Must Remember This . . .

√   That laryngitis can be caused by allergies, viral and bacterial infections, and vocal strain. For a proper diagnosis, see your doctor. Antibiotics are only effective against bacterial infections. Unless your doctor advises you to do so, don't take them for anything else.

√   That using a humidifier and drinking lots of water are the best ways to prevent winter throat problems.

√   That over-the-counter nasal sprays should be used with caution. But certain prescription-only nasal sprays can actually help prevent allergy attacks before they occur.

√   That habitual throat clearing is bad for the voice. It's better to clear your throat by swallowing.

Epilogue

I opened my mail today and found a letter from a national magazine with a compelling appeal: "Tired of reading about one travesty of justice after another, and not knowing what to do about it?" It urged me to subscribe to their bulletin of contact numbers for corporate bullies, key legislators, and grass roots organizations. But what really caught my eye was the headline on the reply card:

"IT'S YOUR VOICE-USE IT!"

Now that you have gained the skills in this book and discovered the power in your voice, how will you use it? Who will you seek to influence and to what end?

Many things about America today need fixing. Thirty-eight million Americans live in poverty. Fifteen million children are at risk. Add your favorite problem to the list.

But what doesn't need fixing is that we still have the right of free speech. We are not politically repressed. Any one of us is free to express our views on any issue by calling a talk show or an elected representative, speaking out at a school board meeting, engaging in public debate, speaking up at work or speaking words of support to our friends and loved ones.

The right words, powerfully spoken, can change lives. The words of King, Kennedy, Churchill. . . Words spoken to you by a friend that you remember for the rest of your life.

The problem is, too many of us are choosing to remain silent.

In this book I have told you everything I know about improving the sound of your voice and the quality of your communication. If you've felt embarrassed or shy, I hope you now feel confident. If you've felt fear, I hope you now feel courage. If you've felt insignificant, I hope you now feel strong. The next step is action.

It's your voice. Use it well.

Appendix A

Publisher's note:
Inclusion in this listing does not constitute an endorsement by the author or publisher. While the information below was current at press time, changes may occur after the book is in print. If you discover a change please notify the publisher so we may keep the next edition current.

Accent Reduction Specialists/ Voice Coaches

California

Cross Currents
Communications
Sheryl Sever
22 1/2 Buena Vista Avenue
San Anselmo, CA 94960
415-485-1217
currentcom@aol.com

Connecticut

Fitzgerald Communication
Janet Fitzgerald
119 Halstead Avenue
Greenwich, CT 06831-4913
203-532-0908
Fax: 203-532-0212
fitzcomco@aol.com

Florida

SmarTalkers
Wendy Warman
314 S. Missouri Ave. Suite 311
Clearwater, FL. 33756-5882
727-441-9858
Fax: 727-461-2727
www.Smartalkers.com

New York

Lynne Friedman
445 East 80th Street
New York NY 10021
212-249-0061

Ohio

Foreign Accent Reduction, Inc.
Susan Lippman Saltzman
15875 Van Aken Blvd., #302C
Shaker Hts., OH 44120
(216) 696-7732

Wisconsin

June Johnson
500 West Bender Road
Suite 67
Milwaukee, WI 53217-4100
800-988-0644
voicepwr1@aol.com

Presentation Skills Trainers & Consultants

Arizona

Marcia Reynolds,
4301 N. 21st St. #56
Phoenix, AZ 85016
888-998-5064
covisioner@aol.com

Seahawk Associates, Inc.
Charlie Hawkins
425 Manzanita Drive
Sedona, AZ 86336
1-888-285-HAWK
seahawk@sedona.net

California

Callback Communications
Janet Keller
4043 Piedmont Avenue #3
Oakland, CA 94611
510-547-3704
Fax: 510-547-7195
asff@slipnet.com

Joel Roberts
Media Training
2263 Fox Hills Drive #302
Los Angeles, CA 90064
310-286-0631

Empowerment Enterprises
Jane Sanders
14020 Captains Row, Suite 307
Marina del Rey, CA
90292-7364
310-306-4546
Fax: 310-827-0776
www.speaking.com/
sanders.html

Patricia Fripp
527 Hugo Street
San Francisco, CA 94122
(415) 753-6556
(800) 634-3035
www.fripp.com

Dr. Marilyn Manning
945 Mountain View Avenue
Mountain View, CA. 94040
650-965-3663
Fax: 650-965-3668
www.mmanning.com

PROCOACH
Bill Cole
1523 Alma Terrace
San Jose, CA 95125
408-294-2776
Fax: 408-298-9525
procoachbc@aol.com

Booher Consultants, Inc.
Rachel Lane
4001 Gateway Drive
Colleyville, TX 76034
817-868-1200 ext. 100
www.booherconsultants.com

ViewPoint Consultation &
Seminars
Dr. Cecelia J. Soares
2757 West Newell Avenue
Walnut Creek, CA 94595
800-883-2181
Fax: 925-935-1682
CeceliaSoares@worldnet.att.net

Connecticut

Brian Judd
Media Training
PO Box 715
Avon, CT 06001
800-562-4357

LJL Seminars
Lenny Laskowski

106 Schoolhouse Road
Newington, CT. 06111-4002
860-666-4855
1-800-606-4855
www.ljlseminars.com

Florida

Motivational Training Center
M. Tina Dupree
P.O. Box 540821
Opa Locka, FL 33054
305-685-0074
Fax: 305-769-1005
www.thechickenlady.com

Indiana

Real-Impact
Jean Palmer Heck
1955 Mulsanne Drive
Zionsville, IN 46077-9077
317-873-3772
Fax: 317-873-5949
http://www.Real-Impact.com

Maryland

ebiz
Bob Bailey
528 Ashford Road, Suite 1000
Silver Spring MD 20910
800.707.ebiz

301.587.faxx
www.speakers.com/ebiz.html

Michigan

Radiant Communications
Marlena Reigh
2359 Prairie Street
Ann Arbor, MI 48105
734-668-6074
Fax: 734-663-7190
RadianTalk@aol.com

Missouri

Corporate Communications
Patricia Ball
9875 Northbridge Road
St. Louis, MO 63124
314) 966-5452

Candice Coleman Associates
Candice M. Coleman
1822 Hickory St.
St. Louis, MO 63104-2930
314-621-9228
Fax : 314-621-1203
www.SayItWell.com

New York

Diane DiResta
PO Box 140714
Staten Island NY 10314

718-273-8627
www.diresta.com

Halpern/Gruskay Ltd.
Holly D. Gruskay
32 Runyon Place
Scarsdale, NY 10583
914-632-8870
hgruskay@technologist.com

TJ Walker
Media Training
PO Box 42
Cathedral Station
New York, NY 10025
888-TJ-SPEAK
Fax: 212-661-2399
www.tjwalker.com

Ohio

Patrick J. Donadio
191 West Jeffrey Place
Columbis, OH 43214
614-263-3421
www.Ohiospeakers.com/
pdonadio.html

Pennsylvania

Brody Communications Ltd.
Marjorie Brody, CSP, CMC
P.O. Box 8868
Elkins Park, PA 19027 USA

215- 886-1688
Fax: 215-886-1699
http://www.brodycomm.com

The Executive Image
Linda Blackman
5020 Castleman St.
Pittsburgh, PA 15232-2107
412-682-2200
MsBlackman@aol.com

Tennessee

Executive Communication
Training
Ralph E. Hillman
614 Woodmont Drive
Murfreesboro, TN 37129
615-849-1335
Fax: 615-898-5826
Ralph_Hillman@juno.com

Texas

Elizabeth Brazell Nichols
Brazell Nichols Institute
19 Concord Circle
Austin, TX 78737
512-288-1095
Fax: 512-301-2851
bni@swbell.net

Shirley Markley
PO Box 161842
Austin,TX 78716

512-329-0881
Fax 512-329-5869
shirleymarkley@ibm.net

Speak For Yourself
Karen Cortell Reisman
13210 Laurel Wood
Dallas, TX 75240
972-490-8676
Fax: 972-385-7652

Canada

MHW Communications
Helen Wilkie
Toronto, Canada
416-966-5023
Fax: 416-966-2504
mhwcomm@total.net

Appendix B

For more information about Analytical Trilogy and the work of Dr. Norberto R. Keppe and Dr. Claudia B. Pacheco contact:

The International Society of Analytical Trilogy
Avenida Rebouças 3819
05401 Sao Paulo, SP Brasil

Tel: 011-55-11-210-3616
sitaenk@uol.com.br

Books in English by Drs. Keppe and Pacheco are available in the U.S. through:

Campbell Hall Press
616 East Palisade Avenue
Englewood Cliffs, NJ 07632

Tel: 201-541-8595
books@greatvoice.com

Index

Don't Miss These Audio Tape Programs From Susan Berkley!

Voice Mastery Technique

VoiceShaping®: How To Find Your Million Dollar Voice

In this audio workshop, Susan Berkley shows you how to master the voice control techniques that will help you build your business and close more sales. A great complimentary program to *Speak to Influence*. Based on years of research and experience, VoiceShaping® is an indispensable tool for anyone wanting to become a masterful communicator.   6 audio cassettes, 100 page manual - $99 + $5 s/h

Voice-Over Training

How To Get Your Voice On TV And Radio Commercials: The Complete Guide To Breaking Into Voice-Overs

Have people always commented on the sound of your voice? When you listen to TV and radio commercials and cartoons do you think "I'd love to do that!"? If you are just starting out or curious about the business of voice-over, these tapes are a must. Presented in an informative interview style, Susan Berkley and her guests will explain what you really need to know about the voice-over business, from the experts on the inside. You'll hear from: top New York City casting director Charles Rosen; the owner of L.A.'s premier voice-over recording studio, Mark Graue; and from Susan Berkley herself.
3 audio cassettes - $29.95 + $3 s/h

Make Money Talking Funny: How To Develop Marketable Voices For Cartoons And Animation With GT Cooper

Learn how to turn those funny voices that annoyed your teachers into a lucrative and exciting career. GT Cooper (the voice of Marvel Comics' Captain America) and his guests teach you exactly how to develop and market your character voice talents. Step-by-step instruction makes it easy and fun!   3 audio cassettes -$29.95 + $3 s/h

How To Make Big Money In Voice-Overs

A complete marketing program for anyone who is serious about making voice-over their full time career. Follow in the footsteps of Susan Berkley as she reveals the marketing secrets that allowed her to become one of the nation's most successful female voice-over artists. With this program you'll understand the voice-over business from the inside- out and exactly what to do to succeed.   6 audio cassettes, manual - $99 + $5 s/h

---

Our iron clad money-back guarantee:
Take up to one full year to review these programs.
If you are dissatisfied for any reason, simply return the tapes
in good condition, for a full refund less shipping and handling

---

Order Your Audio Tapes Here Now!

	Quantity	x Price	Total
Voice Mastery Technique			
VoiceShaping®: How To Find Your Million Dollar Voice by Susan Berkley 6 tapes + 100 page manual　　　S&H: $7		$99	
Voice-Over Training			
How To Get Your Voice On TV And Radio Commercials: The Complete Guide To Breaking Into Voice-Overs by Susan Berkley with special guests – 3 tapes		$29.95	
Make Money Talkin' Funny: How To Develop Marketable Voices For Cartoons And Animation with GT Cooper – 3 tapes		$29.95	
How To Make Big Money In Voice-Overs: A Complete Marketing Program For A Successful Voice-Over Career by Susan Berkley 6 tapes + manual		$99	
Subtotal			
Shipping & Handling Tapes: (except VoiceShaping®): $5/first tape set, $3 each additional Overseas and Canada: call for shipping rates			
NJ residents add 6% sales tax			
Total Order			

Name_____

Address_____

City/State/Zip_____

Phone (day)_____email_____

☐ Check enclosed　☐ Visa　☐ MC　☐ Amex

Card #_____ Exp date_____

Name on card:_____

Order now!

Tel: 800-333-8108 or
　　201-541-8595
Fax: (201) 541-8608

We gladly accept:

VISA　MasterCard　AMERICAN EXPRESS

Order on-line:via secure server
http://www.greatvoice.com
email: books@greatvoice.com

Mail: Campbell Hall Press
616 E. Palisade Avenue
Englewood Cliffs, NJ 07632

Order Additional Books Today!

Speak to Influence makes a great gift or training aid!

For additional copies, ask your favorite bookstore or order directly by using this form

	Quantity	x Price	Total
Additional copies of *Speak To Influence*		$14.95	
Quantity discount on orders of 2 or more: 10%			
Subtotal			
Shipping & Handling Books: $4 first book, $1 each additional Overseas and Canada: call for shipping rates			
NJ residents add 6% sales tax $.90 per book or 6% on quantity orders			
Total Order			

Name_____

Address_____

City/State/Zip_____

Phone (day)_____

email_____

☐ Check enclosed ☐ Visa ☐ MC ☐ Amex

Card #_____

Exp date_____

Name on card:_____

Order now!

Tel: 800-333-8108 or
201-541-8595

Fax: (201) 541-8608

We gladly accept:

VISA   MasterCard   AMERICAN EXPRESS

Order on-line via secure server
http://www.greatvoice.com

or email: books@greatvoice.com

Mail:
Campbell Hall Press
616 E. Palisade Avenue
Englewood Cliffs, NJ 07632

Get a FREE
LIFETIME SUBSCRIPTION
To "The VoiceCoach"
On-Line Newsletter

Just for buying this book!

Speak with confidence! **"The VoiceCoach"** is a FREE electronic newsletter (E-zine) dedicated to helping you become a more compelling speaker over the phone or face-to-face. Every month Susan Berkley brings you the latest speaking tips and powerful presentation techniques. This free subscription offer is available by email only. We do not distribute the VoiceCoach by postal mail or fax.

Subscribe today!
Just point your browser to:

www.greatvoice.com

While you're there, check out **"The VoiceCoach"** archives and down-load back issues of the newsletter absolutely free!

Publishers note:
We value our subscribers and their need for confidentiality. By subscribing to "The VoiceCoach," your name and email address will be held in strictest confidence and will never be sold or otherwise redistributed.